New Inside Out

Sue Kay & Vaughan Jones
with Peter Maggs & Catherine Smith

Elementary

Student's Book

WB = **Workbook**. Each unit of the Workbook contains a one-page section which develops practical writing skills.

1 Airport

Grammar *be:* present simple affirmative. Nouns. *a/an. this/these*
Vocabulary Countries. Nationalities. Languages. Common objects. Numbers *0–10*
Useful phrases Asking for clarification

Listening

1 🌐 **1.01 Read and listen to the conversation. Answer the questions.**
a) What's his name? b) What's her name?

Mike: Hi. I'm Mike. What's your name?
Helen: Oh, hello. I'm Helen.
Mike: Nice to meet you.

Listen and repeat.

2 🌐 **1.02 Read and listen to the conversation. Answer the questions.**
a) Where's she from?   b) Where's he from?

Mike: Are you American?
Helen: No, I'm not. I'm British. I'm from London.
Mike: Oh, I love London. It's my favourite city.
Helen: Where are you from?
Mike: I'm from New York.

Listen and repeat.

Speaking

Introduce yourself to people in the class.

> Hi. I'm Rosa.
> What's your name?

> I'm Jon.

> Nice to meet you.
> Where are you from?

> I'm from Bilbao.

Vocabulary

1 ✹ 1.03 **Listen and repeat the country and nationality words. <u>Underline</u> the stressed syllables.**

Country	Nationality	Language
I'm from …	*I'm …*	*I speak …*
Bra<u>zil</u>	Bra<u>zil</u>ian	(1) Portu<u>guese</u>
<u>Ger</u>many	<u>Ger</u>man	(2) <u>Ger</u>man
Italy	Italian	(3) _____
Russia	Russian	(4) _____
Poland	Polish	(5) _____
Spain	Spanish	(6) _____
China	Chinese	(7) _____
Japan	Japanese	(8) _____

2 ✹ 1.04 **Listen and number (*1–6*) the languages as you hear them.**

Italian ☐   Russian ☐   Polish ☐   Spanish ☐ *1*   Chinese ☐   Japanese ☐

3 **Complete the language words in the table in Exercise 1. <u>Underline</u> the stressed syllables.**

✹ 1.05 **Listen, check and repeat.**

4 **Say a country. Your partner says the nationality and the language.**

China

Chinese, Chinese

Grammar

be

I'm	I am
You're	You are
He's	He is
She's	She is
It's	It is
We're	We are
They're	They are

Is he Spanish?
Yes, he **is**.

1 **Complete the questions and answers for the pictures (*a–f*).**

a) 'Is he Chinese?'   'Yes, *he is*.'
b) '*Are* _____ Spanish?'   'Yes, *they* _____ .'
c) '_____ *it* Japanese?'   'Yes, _____ .'
d) '_____ Russian?'   'Yes, _____ .'
e) '_____ Polish?'   'Yes, _____ .'
f) '_____ British?'   'Yes, _____ .'

2 ✹ 1.06 **Listen, check and repeat.**

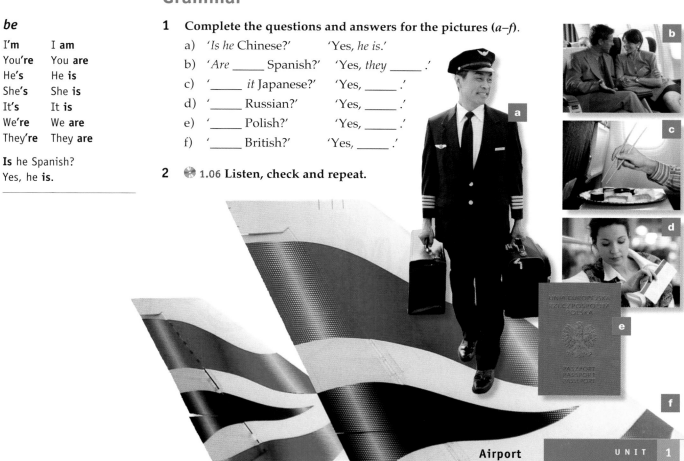

Vocabulary & Listening

1 🎧 1.07 **Listen and repeat the words (1–12).**

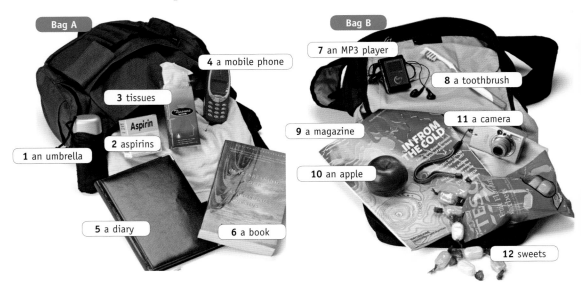

Bag A
1 an umbrella
2 aspirins
3 tissues
4 a mobile phone
5 a diary
6 a book

Bag B
7 an MP3 player
8 a toothbrush
9 a magazine
10 an apple
11 a camera
12 sweets

2 🎧 1.08 **Read and listen to the conversations. Which is Mike's bag? Which is Helen's bag?**

1

Customs:	Right. What's in your bag, sir?
Mike:	Oh, um, a magazine, a camera, an apple, a toothbrush …
Customs:	And what's this, sir?
Mike:	Oh, it's an MP3 player.
Customs:	Hm. And what are these?
Mike:	They're sweets.

2

Customs:	What's in your bag, madam?
Helen:	A book, an umbrella, tissues, a diary …
Customs:	And what's this?
Helen:	It's a mobile phone.
Customs:	And what are these?
Helen:	They're aspirins.

3 **Work with a partner. Practise the conversations.**

Grammar

Nouns

Singular

What's **this**?
It's **a** book. /
It's **an** umbrella.

Consonant sound
= **a** (a pen)
Vowel sound (a, e, i, o, u)
= **an** (an apple)

Plural

What are **these**?
They're book**s**.

1 **Complete the table.**

Singular	Plural
an aspirin	(1) *aspirins*
(2) _____	apples
(3) _____	diaries
(4) _____	toothbrushes

🎧 1.09 **Listen, check and repeat.**

2 **Look at the pictures (a–f). Write questions and answers with *this/it* and *these/they*.**

a) What's this? It's a diary.

a diary   pens   keys   coins   a bag   watches

🎧 1.10 **Listen, check and repeat.**

3 Grammar *Extra* 1 page 126. Read the explanation and do the exercises.

Pronunciation

The alphabet

Sounds Letters

Sounds	Letters
/eɪ/	A H J K
/iː/	B C D E G P T V
/e/	F L M N S X Z
/aɪ/	I Y
/əʊ/	O
/uː/	Q U W
/ɑː/	R

1 🔊 1.11 Listen and repeat the vowels *A, E, I, O, U*.

2 🔊 1.12 Listen and repeat the consonants and vowels.

3 🔊 1.13 Listen and write the order in which you hear these groups of vowels.

a) A E I O U ☐   d) I A O U E ☐

b) A I O E U ☐   e) I U A O E ☐

c) E I A U O ☐ 1

Vocabulary

Numbers

0 = oh (zero)
1 = one
2 = two
3 = three
4 = four
5 = five
6 = six
7 = seven
8 = eight
9 = nine
10 = ten

01662 345789 =
oh one double six two
three four five
seven eight nine

1 🔊 1.14 Listen and repeat the numbers.

2 🔊 1.15 Listen and complete the London telephone numbers for these airlines.

a) Air France: 0870 142 4 3 4 3   d) American Airlines: 020 7365 _____

b) British Airways: 0870 850 _____   e) China Airlines: 020 8745 _____

c) Lufthansa: _____ 837 7747   f) Japan Airlines: _____

Say a number. Your partner says the airline.

3 | **Pairwork** **Student A:** page 116 **Student B:** page 121

Listening & Speaking

1 Complete the conversation with the information in the box.

> 020 7653 2001   It's helen21@hotpost.com   Taylor. T–A–Y–L–O–R.

Helen: Goodbye, Mike.
Mike: Um, can I see you in London?
Helen: Yes. Phone me.
Mike: OK. What's your surname?
Helen: (1) _____ .
Mike: What's your phone number?
Helen: (2) _____ .
Mike: What's your email address?
Helen: (3) _____ .
Mike: OK, bye, Helen. See you.

🔊 1.16 Listen, check and repeat.

Work with a partner. Practise the conversation.

2 Ask three people the questions in Exercise 1.

Useful phrases

1 🔘 **1.17 Read, listen and complete the conversation with** *say, spell* **or** *repeat*.

Student: How do you (1) *say* 'Francia' in English?
Teacher: 'France'.
Student: How do you (2) _____ it?
Teacher: F–R–A–N–C–E.
Student: Ah, yes. 'France'. How do you (3) _____ 'Italia' in English?
Teacher: 'Italy'.
Student: How do you (4) _____ it?
Teacher: I–T–A–L–Y.
Student: Oh yes. 'Italy'. English is easy. How do you (5) _____ 'Alemania'?
Teacher: 'Germany'.
Student: Sorry?
Teacher: 'Germany'.
Student: How do you (6) _____ it?
Teacher: G–E–R–M–A–N–Y.
Student: Can you (7) _____ that, please?
Teacher: G–E–R–M–A–N–Y.
Student: OK, thanks.

2 🔘 **1.18 Listen and repeat the useful phrases.**

a) How do you say 'Francia' in English?
b) How do you spell it?
c) Sorry?
d) Can you repeat that, please?
e) OK, thanks.

3 🔘 **1.19 Listen and repeat the words.**

English	Your language
a) <u>pi</u>zza	
b) <u>co</u>ffee	
c) cake	
d) ho<u>tel</u>	
e) bank	
f) <u>lib</u>rary	

Translate the words into your language.

4 Work with a partner. Write a similar conversation with words from Exercise 3. Practise the conversation.

Vocabulary *Extra*

Common nouns

1 Match the pictures with the words.

Singular	Plural
10 _____	aspirins
1 a bag	_____
☐ a _____	children
☐ a <u>diary</u>	_____
☐ an MP<u>3 player</u>	_____
☐ a _____	keys
☐ a maga<u>zine</u>	_____
☐ a man	_____
☐ a <u>mobile phone</u>	_____
☐ a _____	<u>people</u>
☐ a _____	sweets
☐ a _____	<u>tissues</u>
☐ a <u>toothbrush</u>	_____
☐ an um<u>brella</u>	_____
☐ a watch	_____
☐ a <u>woman</u>	_____

2 Complete the singular or plural forms in Exercise 1.

3 Work with a partner. Cover the words and look at the pictures. Ask and answer questions.

> What's this?

> It's a bag.

> What are these?

> They're keys.

Focus on instructions (1)

1 Match the pictures with the phrases.

- 3 Listen to the conversation.
- ☐ Look at the board.
- ☐ Read the text.
- ☐ Work with a partner.
- ☐ Write your name on a piece of paper.
- ☐ Use a dictionary.

2 Complete the instructions with verbs from Exercise 1.

a) *Read* the article.

b) _____ at the photo on page 9.

c) _____ a piece of paper.

d) _____ to the song.

e) _____ in groups of three.

f) _____ the answers to the questions.

2 People

Grammar Possessive determiners. *be*: present simple
Vocabulary Favourite things. Numbers *11–999*. Jobs
Useful phrases Greetings and introductions

Vocabulary

1 Complete the table about Brad Pitt's favourite things. Use the headings in the box.

> Actor   Animal   Drink   Film   Food
> Singer   Sport   Writer

Brad Pitt's favourite things

a) *Actor*:   Dianne Wiest
b) _____ : Jimi Hendrix, Bob Marley
c) _____ : *Planet of the Apes*, *Saturday Night Fever*
d) _____ : Cormac McCarthy
e) _____ : pizza
f) _____ : beer, coffee
g) _____ : cycling, tennis
h) _____ : dogs

🔘 1.20 **Listen and check.**

2 Use the headings in Exercise 1 and make lists with the things in the box.

> cats   Christina Aguilera   Coke   Dan Brown   football   ~~Gwyneth Paltrow~~
> horses   JK Rowling   Johnny Depp   Louis Armstrong   *Mission Impossible*
> pasta   *Star Wars*   steak   swimming   tea

Actor	Singer	Film	Writer	Food	Drink	Sport	Animal
Gwyneth Paltrow							

Add your favourite things to the lists above.

Speaking

Ask your partner about his or her favourite things. Use *Who …?* for people or *What …?* for things.

> Who's your favourite singer?

> Beyoncé.

> What's your favourite sport?

> Skiing.

Grammar

Subject pronoun	Possessive determiner
I	my
you	your
he	his
she	her
it	its
we	our
they	their

1 Complete the sentences with a possessive determiner.

a) I'm an actor. *My* favourite singers are Jimi Hendrix and Bob Marley.

b) He's the Prince of Wales. _____ wife is called Camilla.

c) She's from Los Angeles. _____ films include *Tomb Raider* and *Mr & Mrs Smith*.

d) We're married. _____ names are Bill and Hillary.

e) They're Spanish. _____ surname is Iglesias.

🌐 **1.21 Listen and check.**

2 Work with a partner. Who are the people in Exercise 1?

Vocabulary

Numbers

11 = e<u>le</u>ven
12 = twelve
13 = thir<u>teen</u>
14 = four<u>teen</u>
15 = fif<u>teen</u>
16 = six<u>teen</u>
17 = seven<u>teen</u>
18 = eigh<u>teen</u>
19 = nine<u>teen</u>

20 = <u>twenty</u>
30 = <u>thirty</u>
40 = <u>forty</u>
50 = <u>fifty</u>
60 = <u>sixty</u>
70 = <u>seventy</u>
80 = <u>eighty</u>
90 = <u>ninety</u>
100 = one <u>hun</u>dred

1 🌐 **1.22 Listen and repeat the numbers.**

2 🌐 **1.23 Listen and circle the numbers you hear. Repeat the numbers.**

a) (13) / 30   b) 14 / 40   c) 15 / 50   d) 16 / 60   e) 17 / 70   f) 18 / 80   g) 19 / 90

3 Write the numbers in numerals.

a) seven   *7*
b) twenty-eight
c) forty-seven
d) sixty-five
e) one hundred and ten
f) two hundred and forty-five

🌐 **1.24 Listen and repeat.**

4 Work with a partner. Use the numbers in Exercise 3 to complete the information.

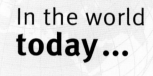

In the world **today...**

a) *28*% of people are under 15 years old.

b) _____% of people are between 15 and 64 years old.

c) _____% of people are over 65 years old.

d) _____% of people live in cities.

e) _____ people are born every 60 seconds.

f) _____ people die every 60 seconds.

🌐 **1.25 Listen and check.**

Speaking

1 Match an age from the box with a person in the photos below. Discuss with a partner.

46 58 19 72 9 41 5 64 23 7 35 29

2 Write the ages in words.

a) She's twenty-nine.   b) He's ...

🌐 **1.26 Listen and check your ideas.**

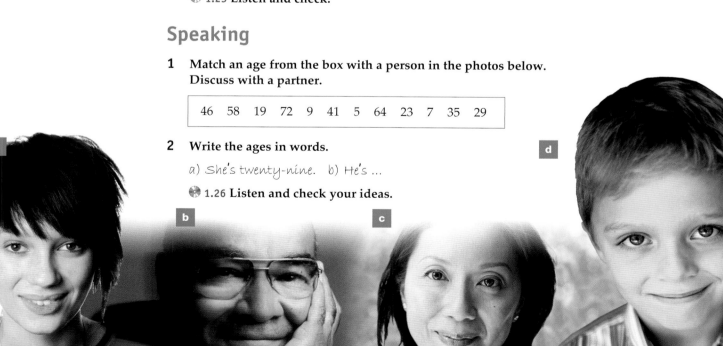

People   UNIT 2   11

Vocabulary

1 **Match the jobs with the photos.**

> a doctor   a hairdresser   an IT technician   a lawyer   a sales manager   nurses
> shop assistants   a taxi driver

Write sentences.

a) He's a lawyer.   b) She's a hairdresser.   c) They're shop assistants.

🌐 **1.27 Listen, check and repeat.**

2 **Work with a partner. Look at the information about the percentage of women in different jobs in the UK. Match each job with one of the percentages in the box.**

> 8%   ~~25%~~   32%   ~~39%~~   42%   73%   83%   89%

The percentage of **women** in
these jobs
in the UK

a) sales managers 25%
b) doctors 39%
c) nurses
d) lawyers
e) IT technicians
f) hairdressers
g) shop assistants
h) taxi drivers

🌐 **1.28 Listen and check your ideas. Are the percentages similar in your country?**

Pronunciation

1 **Complete the table with jobs from the box.**

> actor   doctor   English teacher   IT technician   singer   student
> university professor   writer

A: *an* with vowel sounds	B: *a* with consonant sounds
an actor	*a doctor*

2 🌐 **1.29 Listen, check and repeat.**

Grammar

be

Affirmative	Negative
I'm	I'm not
You're	You aren't
He's	He isn't
She's	She isn't
It's	It isn't
We're	We aren't
They're	They aren't

(aren't = are not
isn't = is not)

Are you married?
Yes, I am.
No, I'm not.

1 Work with a partner. Make true sentences with the correct affirmative or negative forms of *be*.

a) George Bush *is* from Texas. He *isn't* from California.
b) Domenico Dolce and Stefano Gabbana _____ Spanish. They _____ Italian.
c) Isabel Allende _____ an artist. She _____ a writer.
d) The White House _____ in New York. It _____ in Washington.
e) The Petronas Towers _____ in Kuala Lumpur. They _____ in Hong Kong.
f) LOT _____ a Polish airline. It _____ a German airline.

🔘 **1.30 Listen and check.**

2 Complete the questions and answers.

a) '*Are* you a university student?'   'Yes, *I am.*'   'No, *I'm not.*'
b) '*Are* you 21?   'Yes, _____ .'   'No, _____ .'
c) '*Is* your mother a taxi driver?'   'Yes, _____ .'   'No, _____ .'
d) '_____ your father over 65 years old?'   '_____ .'   '_____ .'
e) '_____ your favourite drink Coke?'   '_____ .'   '_____ .'
f) '_____ your grandparents from here?'   '_____ .'   '_____ .'

🔘 **1.31 Listen, check and repeat.**

3 Work with a partner. Ask and answer the questions in Exercise 2.

4 Grammar *Extra* 2 page 126. Read the explanation and do the exercises.

Writing & Speaking

1 Write the questions in the correct order. Use contractions where possible.

a) What / surname / your / is ? *What is your surname? / What's your surname?*
b) How / you / old / are ?
c) What / email address / is / your ?
d) What / your / is / first name ?
e) What / mobile number / is / your ?
f) What / your / home phone number / is ?
g) Where / from / you / are ?
h) What / your / is / job ?

🔘 **1.32 Listen, check and repeat.**

2 Work with a partner. Match the information in the Dateline Profile with the questions in Exercise 1.

1   Rachel ➔ d) What's your first name?
2   Green ➔ a) What's your surname?

3 Pairwork **Student A:** page 116 **Student B:** page 121

Useful phrases

1 Read and complete the conversations with the words and phrases in the box.

> ~~I'm very well~~   Goodbye   Fine   Good morning   Nice to meet you
> how are you

Cathy: Hello, Mrs Jones.
Mrs Jones: Hello, dear. How are you?
Cathy: (1) *I'm very well*, thank you.
             And (2) _____ ?
Mrs Jones: Oh, not too bad, thank you, dear.

Andy: Hi! How are you?
Beth: (3) _____ , thanks. And you?
Andy: Not too bad.
Beth: Sorry – I'm in a hurry!
Andy: Oh, OK. Bye.
Beth: See you.

David: (4) _____ . I'm David Grant.
Erica: Nice to meet you, David. I'm Erica.
David: (5) _____ , Erica.
Erica: And this is Frank, my assistant.
David: Hello, Frank. Nice to meet you.

Newsagent: Good afternoon, sir. That's £1.
Man: Thank you.
Newsagent: Thank you very much, sir.
             (6) _____ .
Man: Goodbye.

🔘 **1.33 Listen and check.**

2 Complete the table of useful phrases with the headings in the box.

> ~~Saying hello~~   Saying goodbye   Introducing people   Greeting people

1 *Saying hello*	2 _____	3 _____	4 _____
Hello.	How are you?	This is Frank.	Bye.
Hi!	I'm very well, thank you.	Nice to meet you.	See you.
Good morning.	Fine thanks. And you?		Goodbye.
Good afternoon.	Not too bad.		

🔘 **1.34 Listen, check and repeat the useful phrases**.

3 Practise the conversations in Exercise 1 with a partner.

Vocabulary *Extra*

Jobs

1 Match the pictures with the jobs.

- [10] an <u>ac</u>tor
- [ ] a <u>doc</u>tor
- [ ] a <u>hair</u>dresser
- [ ] an <u>IT</u> tech<u>ni</u>cian
- [ ] a <u>law</u>yer
- [ ] a nurse
- [ ] a <u>sales</u> <u>ma</u>nager
- [ ] a <u>shop</u> as<u>sis</u>tant
- [ ] a <u>sin</u>ger
- [ ] a <u>ta</u>xi <u>dri</u>ver
- [ ] a <u>wai</u>ter
- [ ] a <u>wri</u>ter

2 Work with a partner. Cover the words and look at the pictures. Ask and answer questions.

> What does he do?

> He's a taxi driver.

3 Think about your family and friends. Write their jobs in English.

Focus on countries and nationalities

1 Complete the table. <u>Underline</u> the stressed syllables.

Flag	Country	Nationality	Language	Flag	Country	Nationality	Language
	Bra<u>zil</u>	(1) *Bra<u>zi</u>lian*	Portu<u>guese</u>		Poland	(10) _____	(11) _____
	(2) _____	Chinese	(3) _____		(12) _____	Russian	(13) _____
	Germany	(4) _____	(5) _____		Spain	(14) _____	(15) _____
	(6) _____	Italian	(7) _____		the UK *	British	(16) _____
	(8) _____	(9) _____	Japanese		the USA	(17) _____	(18) _____

*Note: The United Kingdom (the UK) = England, Scotland, Wales and Northern Ireland. Great Britain = England, Scotland and Wales.

2 Write down three other countries you know with their nationality and language. How do you say them in English? Add them to the table.

3 Family

Grammar Possessive 's/s'. Present simple affirmative
Vocabulary Family
Useful phrases Advice and warnings

Reading

1 🌐 1.35 **Read the description of the Collister families. Name each person in the photograph.**

Meet the Collisters

Peter Collister and John Collister are identical twin brothers.

Peter is married to Pauline, and John is married to Pat. Pauline and Pat are sisters. Peter and Pauline have one daughter and one son. Jennifer is nine and Joe is six. John and Pat have two sons and one daughter. Tom is nine. Jack is six. Kitty is four.

a) *Joe*
b) _____
c) _____
d) _____
e) _____
f) _____
g) _____
Peter
John

2 **Do you know any twin brothers or sisters? Tell your partner about them.**

Vocabulary

1 **Complete the information about the Collister families with names from the box.**

Jennifer	Joe	John	Kitty	Pat	~~Pauline~~	Peter	~~Tom~~

Family relation	**Example**
a) husband and wife	Peter and *Pauline*
b) father and son	John and *Tom*
c) mother and daughter	Pat and _____
d) sister and brother	Jennifer and _____
e) uncle and nephew	_____ and Joe
f) aunt and niece	_____ and Jennifer
g) cousin and cousin	_____ or Joe, and Jack
h) brother-in-law and sister-in-law	_____ and Pat

2 🌐 1.36 **Listen, check and repeat.**

Reading

1 Read the descriptions of members of the Collister families. Identify the people.

a)
John is my <u>father</u>.
Pat is my <u>mother</u>.
I have two <u>brothers</u>
called Tom and Jack.

Who am I? *I'm Kitty.*

b)
John is her
<u>husband</u>. Peter
is her <u>brother-in-
law</u>. She has three
<u>children</u>.

Who is she?

c)
Pauline is his **wife**.
Pat is his <u>sister-in-law</u>.
He has one **niece**.

Who is he?

d)
John and Pat are
our <u>parents</u>. Peter
is our <u>uncle</u>, and
Pauline is our **aunt**.
We have one <u>sister</u>
and two <u>cousins</u>.

Who are we?

e)
Joe is their
<u>nephew</u>. Jennifer
is their niece.
They have two
sons and one
<u>daughter</u>.

Who are they?

🌐 **1.37 Listen and check.**

2 Pairwork **Student A:** page 116 **Student B:** page 121

3 Draw your family tree. Tell your partner about people in your family.

> This is my father. His name is Alfio. He's 49.
> He's from Perugia. He's a doctor ...

Grammar

Possessive 's/s'

His father**'s** name is Peter.
(*father* is singular.)

Her brother**s'** names are
Tom and Jack.
(*brothers* is plural.)

1 Who says it? Match the sentences with the names.

a) 'My wife's name is Pauline.' ——— Pat
b) 'My sister's name is Pat.' John and Pat
c) 'My sister's name is Jennifer.' Peter
d) 'My husband's name is John.' Pauline
e) 'My brothers' names are Tom and Jack.' Joe
f) 'Our nephew's name is Joe.' Kitty

🌐 **1.38 Listen and check.**

2 Grammar *Extra* 3 page 126. Read the explanation and do the exercises.

Writing

Write five sentences about names in your family.

1   My mother's name is Pietra.
2   My cousins' names are Tizio, Caio and Adriana ...

Compare your sentences with your partner.

Family

Reading

1 🌐 **1.39 Read about a TV show called *Wife Exchange*. Underline *Margaret* or *Caroline*.**

a) **<u>Margaret</u> / Caroline** is Andy's wife.

b) **Margaret / Caroline** lives with Paul's family for two weeks in *Wife Exchange*.

c) **Margaret / Caroline** eats meals with her family in the kitchen.

d) **Margaret's / Caroline's** children go to bed very late.

e) **Margaret / Caroline** is Paul's wife.

f) **Margaret / Caroline** lives with Andy's family for two weeks in *Wife Exchange*.

g) **Margaret / Caroline** eats meals with her family in front of the TV.

h) **Margaret's / Caroline's** children watch TV in their bedrooms.

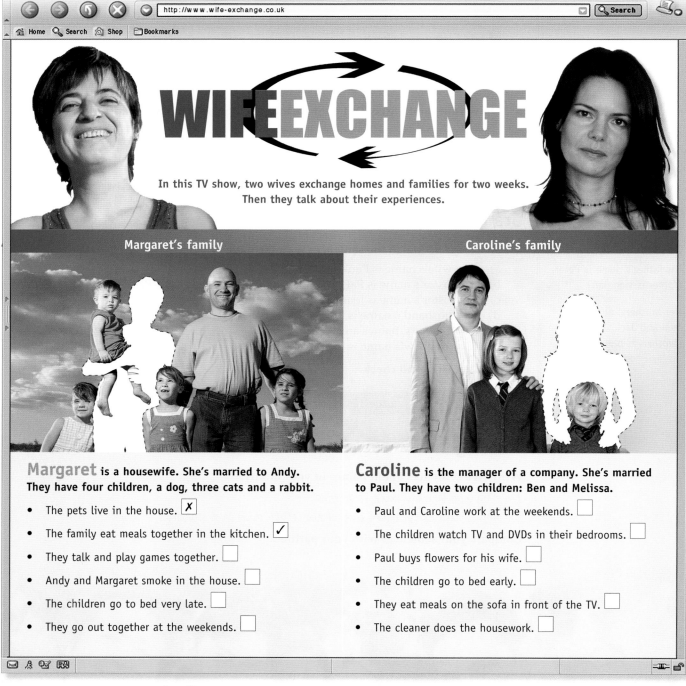

http://www.wife-exchange.co.uk

WIFE EXCHANGE

In this TV show, two wives exchange homes and families for two weeks.
Then they talk about their experiences.

Margaret's family   **Caroline's family**

Margaret is a housewife. She's married to Andy.
They have four children, a dog, three cats and a rabbit.

- The pets live in the house. **✗**
- The family eat meals together in the kitchen. **✓**
- They talk and play games together. ☐
- Andy and Margaret smoke in the house. ☐
- The children go to bed very late. ☐
- They go out together at the weekends. ☐

Caroline is the manager of a company. She's married
to Paul. They have two children: Ben and Melissa.

- Paul and Caroline work at the weekends. ☐
- The children watch TV and DVDs in their bedrooms. ☐
- Paul buys flowers for his wife. ☐
- The children go to bed early. ☐
- They eat meals on the sofa in front of the TV. ☐
- The cleaner does the housework. ☐

2 🌐 **1.40 Listen to Caroline speaking about Margaret's family and Margaret speaking about Caroline's family. Put a cross (✗) next to the things they think are bad, and put a tick (✓) next to the things they think are good.**

3 Compare your answers with a partner. Do you agree with Caroline and Margaret?

Grammar

Present simple: affirmative forms

I
You
We   **work.**
They

He
She   **work**s.
It

1 Write the *he, she, it* forms of these verbs.

a) have *has*   c) do   e) live   g) buy

b) go   d) eat   f) play   h) watch

🔊 1.41 **Listen, check and repeat.**

2 Complete the sentences with the correct form of the verbs in Exercise 1.

a) My parents *live* in a big apartment.

b) My mother _____ to bed early.

c) My father _____ flowers for my mother.

d) I _____ one sister and one brother.

e) My brother _____ games on his computer.

f) My sister _____ TV in her bedroom.

g) We _____ meals together in the kitchen.

h) The cleaner _____ the housework.

🔊 1.42 **Listen, check and repeat.**

Write three sentences about your own family.

Pronunciation

1 🔊 1.43 **Listen to the chants. Circle the ending sound** /s/, /z/ **or** /ɪz/.

A: /s/ /z/ /ɪz/   **B:** /s/ /z/ /ɪz/   **C:** /s/ /z/ /ɪz/

She eats.   She knows.   She dances.

He drinks.   He plays.   He boxes.

She talks.   She goes.   She teaches.

He thinks.   He stays.   He watches.

2 Listen and practise the chants.

Speaking: anecdote

1 🔊 1.44 **Listen to Sophie talking about her favourite relative.** <u>Underline</u> **the correct information.**

a) 'My favourite relative is my <u>cousin</u> / **brother** / **uncle**.'

b) 'His name is **Samuel** / **Daniel** / **Matthew**.'

c) 'He's **24** / **34** / **44** years old.'

d) 'He lives in **New York** / **London** / **Los Angeles**.'

e) 'He's **married** / **single**.'

f) 'He has two cats. Their names are **Romeo and Juliet** / **Coke and Pepsi** / **Champagne and Caviar**.'

g) 'He's a **photographer** / **lawyer** / **teacher**.'

h) 'He works for *Hello* **magazine** / *People* **magazine** / *Heat* **magazine**.'

2 Think about your favourite relative. Write similar sentences about him or her.

Tell your partner about your favourite relative.

> My favourite relative is ...

Useful phrases

1 Complete the useful phrases in *a–d* with the verbs in the box.

be   Call   ~~Drive~~   Have   Smile   worry

a '*Drive* carefully. Don't _____ late.'

b '_____ ! Say cheese!'

c 'Don't _____ ! He's OK.'

d '_____ a good time. Take care. _____ me.'

🌐 **1.45** Listen, check and repeat the useful phrases.

2 Read the conversation. Cross out *Don't* where necessary.

Sally: Bye, Mum. Bye, Dad.
Dad: (1) ~~Don't~~ **drive carefully**.
Sally: (2) **Don't worry**, Dad.
Mum: (3) **Don't have a good time** in Paris.
Sally: Thanks, Mum.
Dad: (4) **Don't forget** your phone.
Sally: OK. My phone's in my bag.
Mum: (5) **Don't call us.** (6) **Don't take care.**
Sally: OK. Bye. See you!

🌐 **1.46** Listen, check and repeat.

Work in groups of three. Practise the conversation.

Vocabulary *Extra*

Family

1 Look at the family tree. Use the words in the box to complete the sentences.

> ~~mother~~ ~~father~~ husband wife
> brother sister son daughter
> aunt uncle niece nephew
> brother-in-law sister-in-law
> grandson granddaughter cousin

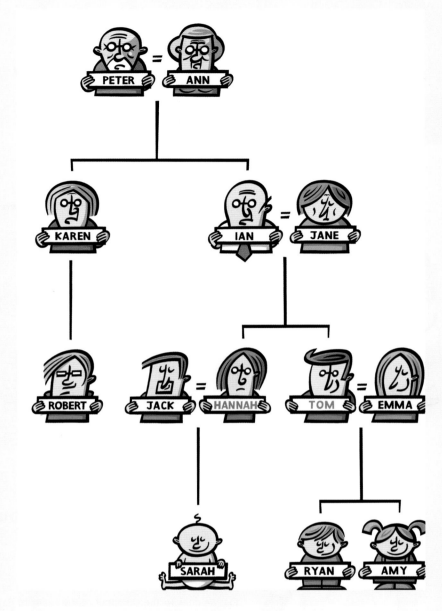

Who is Tom?

a) Tom is Ryan and Amy's *father*.

b) Tom is Hannah's _____ .

c) Tom is Ian and Jane's _____ .

d) Tom is Jack's _____ .

e) Tom is Karen's _____ .

f) Tom is Sarah's _____ .

g) Tom is Emma's _____ .

h) Tom is Robert's _____ .

i) Tom is Peter and Ann's _____ .

Who is Hannah?

j) Hannah is Sarah's *mother*.

k) Hannah is Tom's _____ .

l) Hannah is Ian and Jane's _____ .

m) Hannah is Emma's _____ .

n) Hannah is Karen's _____ .

o) Hannah is Ryan and Amy's _____ .

p) Hannah is Jack's _____ .

q) Hannah is Robert's _____ .

r) Hannah is Peter and Ann's _____ .

2 Who are you? Write similar sentences beginning *I am ...* Use as many family words as possible.

I am André and Monique's son.

I am Chantelle's brother.

I am ...

Focus on numbers

1 Write the numbers.

11 = *eleven*	20 = *twenty*	121 = *one hundred and twenty-one*
12 = _____	30 = _____	257 = _____
13 = _____	40 = _____	376 = _____
14 = _____	50 = _____	492 = _____
15 = _____	60 = _____	533 = _____
16 = _____	70 = _____	648 = _____
17 = _____	80 = _____	764 = _____
18 = _____	90 = _____	805 = _____
19 = _____	100 = _____	999 = _____

2 Dictate any three numbers from 1–999 to your partner.

fifty-four

seven hundred and thirty-six

nine hundred and eighty-nine

4 Different

Grammar Present simple. Object pronouns
Vocabulary *like / don't like + ing*
Useful phrases Expressing opinions

Reading

1 Look at the picture and read and complete the article. Use *He* or *She* according to your own ideas.

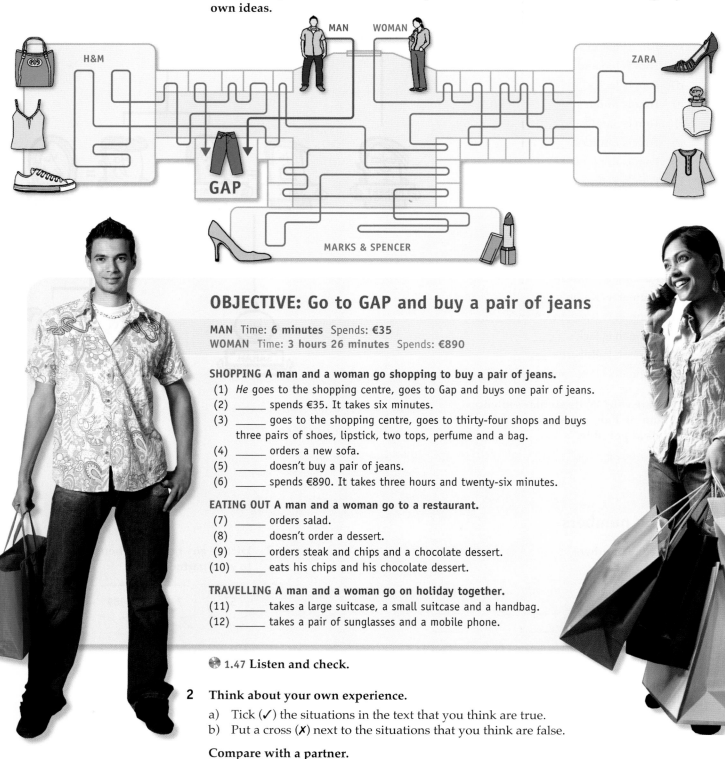

OBJECTIVE: Go to GAP and buy a pair of jeans

MAN Time: **6 minutes** Spends: **€35**
WOMAN Time: **3 hours 26 minutes** Spends: **€890**

SHOPPING A man and a woman go shopping to buy a pair of jeans.
(1) *He* goes to the shopping centre, goes to Gap and buys one pair of jeans.
(2) _____ spends €35. It takes six minutes.
(3) _____ goes to the shopping centre, goes to thirty-four shops and buys three pairs of shoes, lipstick, two tops, perfume and a bag.
(4) _____ orders a new sofa.
(5) _____ doesn't buy a pair of jeans.
(6) _____ spends €890. It takes three hours and twenty-six minutes.

EATING OUT A man and a woman go to a restaurant.
(7) _____ orders salad.
(8) _____ doesn't order a dessert.
(9) _____ orders steak and chips and a chocolate dessert.
(10) _____ eats his chips and his chocolate dessert.

TRAVELLING A man and a woman go on holiday together.
(11) _____ takes a large suitcase, a small suitcase and a handbag.
(12) _____ takes a pair of sunglasses and a mobile phone.

🔊 1.47 Listen and check.

2 Think about your own experience.
a) Tick (✓) the situations in the text that you think are true.
b) Put a cross (✗) next to the situations that you think are false.

Compare with a partner.

Reading & Listening

1 Look at the words in the box. Are men and women's opinions on these topics generally the same or different?

> cars   football   shoes

2 Complete the opinions of the people below with the words from Exercise 1.

How are men and women different?

a) 'I have four pairs of *shoes*. Two pairs for the week. Two pairs for the weekend. My wife has forty pairs of _____ . Maybe fifty! Why?'

b) 'We have two _____ . I drive a VW Golf GTI 2 litre FSI Turbo with alloy wheels. Top speed 200 kilometres an hour. My girlfriend drives a blue car called Fred.'

c) 'Every weekend, my husband goes to the pub and watches _____ on TV. I'm number 3 in his life. Number 1 is _____ . Number 2 is beer ... and number 3 is me!'

🔘 1.48 **Listen and check your answers.**

3 <u>Underline</u> the affirmative or negative form to make true sentences.

a) I **have** / **don't have** forty pairs of shoes.
b) My friends and I **go** / **don't go** to the pub every weekend.
c) My father **watches** / **doesn't watch** football on TV.
d) My mother **has** / **doesn't have** a blue car.
e) I **drive** / **don't drive**.

Compare your sentences with a partner.

Grammar

Present simple

I
You   **work.**
We   **don't work.**
They

Do you **work?**
Yes, I **do.**
No, I **don't.**

He
She   **works.**
It   **doesn't work.**

Does he **work?**
Yes, he **does.**
No, he **doesn't.**

1 Complete the questions and answers.

a) '*Do* you like shopping?'   'Yes, *I do.*'   'No, *I don't.*'
b) '*Does* your father do the housework?'   'Yes, *he does.*'   'No, *he doesn't.*'
c) '*Do* you think about chocolate all the time?'   'Yes, _____ .'   'No, _____ .'
d) '_____ your mother work at the weekend?'   '_____ .'   '_____ .'
e) '_____ you and your friends chat online?'   '_____ .'   '_____ .'
f) '_____ your friends go out a lot?'   '_____ .'   '_____ .'

🔘 1.49 **Listen, check and repeat.**

2 Work with a partner. Ask and answer the questions in Exercise 1.

3 Write true sentences about you from the prompts. Use affirmative or negative forms.

a) work / in a restaurant   c) play / tennis   e) like / flying
   I don't work in a restaurant.   d) speak / Spanish   f) drink / beer
b) sing / in the shower

4 Ask your partner questions using the prompts in Exercise 3. Write the answers.

> Do you work in a restaurant?   No, I don't.

She doesn't work in a restaurant.

5 **Grammar *Extra* 4** page 126. Read the explanation and do the exercises.

Vocabulary & Listening

1 Complete the key with words and phrases from the box.

don't like   don't mind   hate   like   ~~love~~   really like

♥☺   👍☺   ☺   😐   ☹   ☹👎
I (1) *love* it.   I (2) ____ it.   I (3) ____ it.   I (4) ____ it.   I (5) ____ it.   I (6) ____ it.

🔘 **1.50** Listen, check and repeat.

2 Read about Jack and Layla.

Jack loves water, really likes being outside and really likes sport and keeping fit. He hates towns and cities and he doesn't like loud music.

Layla loves spending money. She hates doing housework and she doesn't like cooking. She likes dancing and she doesn't mind loud music. She hates sport.

3 Look at the activities in the box. Put *J* if you think Jack likes it. Put *L* if you think Layla likes it.

clubbing   eating out in restaurants   going to rock concerts   going to the gym
jogging   playing football   shopping   swimming

🔘 **1.51** Listen and check your answers. Are you similar to Jack or Layla?

Speaking

1 Complete the table to show the spelling of the *ing* form.

Most verbs	Verbs ending in *e*	Verbs ending in vowel + consonant
read → *reading*	dance → *dancing*	swim → *swimming*
study → (1) ____	smoke → (3) ____	shop → (5) ____
cook → (2) ____	drive → (4) ____	jog → (6) ____

2 Ask your partner questions. Use the verbs in Exercise 1.

Do you like reading?

Yes, I do. / It's OK. / No, I don't.

3 Pairwork **Student A:** page 117 **Student B:** page 122

Pronunciation

1 Complete the chants with *flying, talking* or *thinking*.

A	B	C
Jogging, walking,	Eating, drinking,	Selling, buying,
Listening, ____ .	Sleeping, ____ .	Sailing, ____ .

2 🔘 **1.52** Listen, check and repeat.

Grammar

Pronouns

Subject	Object
I	me
you	you
he	him
she	her
it	it
we	us
they	them

1 **Complete the sentences with *him, her, it* or *them*.**

a) I don't like the Beatles. Do you like *them*?

b) I don't like Robbie Williams. Do you like _____ ?

c) I don't like Mariah Carey. Do you like _____ ?

d) I don't like Eminem. Do you like _____ ?

e) I don't like the Sugababes. Do you like _____ ?

f) I don't like pop music. Do you like _____ ?

🔘 **1.53 Listen, check and repeat.**

2 **Write some sentences about people or things you don't like.**

I don't like Madonna.   I don't like doing the washing up.

Read your sentences and ask for your partner's opinion.

> I don't like Madonna. Do you like her?

> No, I don't.

Reading & Writing

1 **Read and complete the message with an object pronoun from the box.**

~~me~~ me you him her it it us them them

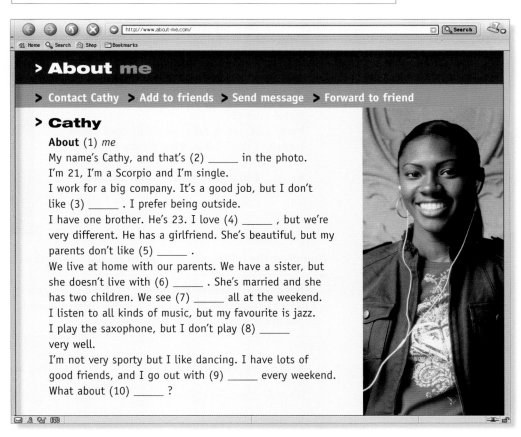

> About me

> Contact Cathy > Add to friends > Send message > Forward to friend

> Cathy

About (1) *me*
My name's Cathy, and that's (2) _____ in the photo.
I'm 21, I'm a Scorpio and I'm single.
I work for a big company. It's a good job, but I don't
like (3) _____ . I prefer being outside.
I have one brother. He's 23. I love (4) _____ , but we're
very different. He has a girlfriend. She's beautiful, but my
parents don't like (5) _____ .
We live at home with our parents. We have a sister, but
she doesn't live with (6) _____ . She's married and she
has two children. We see (7) _____ all at the weekend.
I listen to all kinds of music, but my favourite is jazz.
I play the saxophone, but I don't play (8) _____
very well.
I'm not very sporty but I like dancing. I have lots of
good friends, and I go out with (9) _____ every weekend.
What about (10) _____ ?

🔘 **1.54 Listen and check.**

2 **Write a similar message about you.**

About me My name's Wilfried. That's me in the photo. I'm ...

Useful phrases

1 🌐 **1.55 Read and listen to the conversations. <u>Underline</u> the adjectives you hear.**

a) Ann: What do you think of Beyoncé?
   Bob: I think she's **great / OK / terrible**. What about you?
   Ann: I agree. I really like her.

b) Cathy: What do you think of Jude Law?
   Debra: I think he's **great / OK / terrible**. What about you?
   Cathy: I think he's **great / OK / terrible**, but I prefer Leonardo DiCaprio.

c) Fran: What do you think of the Rolling Stones?
   Greg: I think they're **great / OK / terrible**. What about you?
   Fran: I don't agree. I think they're **great / OK / terrible**.

d) Harry: What do you think of Wayne Rooney?
   Isobel: Who?
   Harry: Wayne Rooney. He's a football player.
   Isobel: I don't know. What do you think of him?
   Harry: I think he's **great / OK / terrible**.

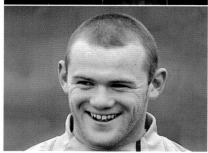

2 **Complete the table with the useful phrases from the conversations.**

> ~~What do you think of Beyoncé?~~   I think she's great.   I think he's OK.
> I prefer Leonardo DiCaprio.   I think they're terrible.
> What about you?   I don't know.

Asking for an opinion	Giving an opinion
What do you think of Beyoncé?	

🌐 **1.56 Listen, check and repeat the useful phrases.**

3 **Circle the adjectives that are true for you in Exercise 1. Practise the conversations with a partner.**

4 **Write a list of your favourite actors, singers, bands and writers.**

   Ask your partner's opinion about the people on your list.

Vocabulary *Extra*

Common verbs

1 Match the pictures with the verbs. Then complete the verb phrases.

- [5] buy *a pair of shoes*
- [ ] drink _____
- [ ] drive _____
- [ ] eat _____
- [ ] live _____
- [ ] play _____
- [ ] smoke _____
- [ ] speak _____
- [ ] spend _____
- [ ] think _____
- [ ] watch _____
- [ ] work _____

2 Work with a partner. Cover the words and look at the pictures. Ask and answer questions.

> What is number 1?

> speak French

French

television

a car

a cigarette

a pair of shoes

about chocolate

beer

football

for a big company

in a big city

$50

chips

Focus on instructions (2)

Complete the instructions with the verbs in the box.

Circle	Complete	Cross out
Match	~~Tick~~	Underline

1 *Tick* the correct sentence.
2 _____ the object pronouns.
3 _____ the subject pronouns.
4 _____ the subject and object pronouns.
5 _____ the list.
6 _____ the incorrect sentence.

[1]
a) He love me.
b) He loves me. ✓

[2]
I love (her) and she loves (me).

[3]
We love them and they love us.

[4]
I → him
you → me
he → her
she → you

[5]
me   you   him
her   it   us   them

[6]
a) I love her.
b) I love she.

Review A

Grammar

▶ Grammar *Extra* pages 126 and 127

1 **Complete the table.**

Subject	Verb (*be*)	Contraction	Question
I	*am*	*I'm*	*Am I …?*
You			
He/She/It			
We			
You			
They			

2 **Complete the conversation with *this* or *these*.**

Officer: Open your bag, please, sir.
Man: Yes, sure.
Officer: What's (1) *this*?
Man: It's an MP3 player.
Officer: Mm. And what are (2) _____ ?
Man: They're tissues.
Officer: Tissues? And what's (3) _____ ?
Man: It's a mobile phone.
Officer: Ah, yes. What's (4) _____ ?
Man: It's a toothbrush.
Officer: Oh, … and what's (5) _____ ?
Man: It's a camera.
Officer: What are (6) _____ ?
Man: They're aspirins. I have a headache.
Officer: Fine. Thank you, sir.

🔵 **1.57 Listen and check.**

3 **Complete the table.**

Subject pronoun	Possessive determiner
I	(1) *my*
(2) _____	your
he	(3) _____
(4) _____	her
it	(5) _____
(6) _____	our
they	(7) _____

4 **Underline the correct answer.**

a) His **sister's** / **sisters'** names are Kate and Amy.
b) My **father's** / **fathers'** name is Ron.
c) Her **son's** / **sons'** wife is Chinese.
d) My **cousin's** / **cousins'** names are Jo and Sara.
e) Their **parent's** / **parents'** names are Sam and Di.
f) My **brother's** / **brothers'** girlfriend is a doctor.

5 **Write questions.**

a) you / work *Do you work?*
b) your mother / like shopping
c) you and your family / eat together every day
d) you / have a Japanese car
e) your father / speak another language
f) you and your friends / go out every night

Answer the questions.

a) Yes, I do.

Compare your answers with a partner.

6 **Complete the sentences with *him*, *her*, *them* or *it*.**

a) Halle Berry is beautiful. I really like *her*.
b) *X-Men* is a bad film. I don't like _____ .
c) Brad Pitt is a very good actor. I really like _____ .
d) The Arctic Monkeys are great. I love _____ .
e) Beyoncé is a good singer, but I don't like _____ .
f) My father is also my friend. I love spending time with _____ .

Tick (✓) the sentences that are true for you.

Compare your answers with a partner.

7 **Spot the mistake! Cross out the incorrect sentence, *a* or *b*.**

1 a) Is she Italian?
   b) ~~She is Italian?~~

2 a) What's this?
   b) What's these?

3 a) Is you're family from Poland?
   b) Is your family from Poland?

4 a) They likes Japanese food.
   b) They like Japanese food.

5 a) He work in a shop.
   b) He works in a shop.

6 a) Do you lives in London?
   b) Do you live in London?

Vocabulary

1 Write the language of each country.

a) [flag] Russia *Russian*

b) [flag] Brazil

c) [flag] Spain

d) [flag] Germany

e) [flag] China

f) [flag] Poland

g) [flag] Italy

h) [flag] Japan

i) [flag] the USA

2 Write the telephone numbers as you say them.

a) 01779 4062 533   *oh one double seven nine, four oh six two, five double three*

b) 05704 294 0056

c) 020 1663 4156

d) 00310 2399 8104

3 Complete the questions with the words in the box.

> ~~actor~~ drink film food singer sport writer

a) 'Who's your favourite *actor*?' 'Tom Cruise.'

b) 'What's your favourite _____ ?' *'The Matrix.'*

c) 'Who's your favourite _____ ?' 'Madonna.'

d) 'What's your favourite _____ ?' 'Milk.'

e) 'What's your favourite _____ ?' 'Chips.'

f) 'Who's your favourite _____ ?' 'Dan Brown.'

g) 'What's your favourite _____ ?' 'Tennis.'

Answer the questions with your own favourites.

Take it in turns to ask and answer the questions with a partner.

4 Write the answers in full.

a) 9 x 5 = *forty-five*

b) 4 + 7 =

c) 15 – 3 =

d) 100 + 5 =

e) 25 + 24 + 25 =

f) 210 – 23 =

g) 131 x 6 =

5 Write vowels (*a, e, i, o, u*) to complete the names of jobs.

a) doctor

b) h_ _ _rdr__ss__r

c) __T t__chn__c__ __n

d) l__wy__r

e) s__l__s m__n__g__r

f) n__rs__

g) sh__p __ss__st__nt

h) t__x__ dr__v__r

6 Complete the sentences with the words in the box.

> don't like   don't mind   hate   ~~like~~   love   really like

♥☺   👍☺   ☺   ☺   ☹   ☹👎

love   hate

a) I ☺ *like* pasta.

b) I ☺ _____ Johnny Depp.

c) I 👍☺ _____ steak.

d) I ☹ _____ swimming.

e) I ♥☺ _____ football.

f) I ☹👎 _____ cats.

Tick (✓) the sentences that are true for you.

Compare your answers with a partner.

7 Look at the family tree and complete the sentences with the words in the box.

> aunt   cousin   ~~husband~~   nephew   niece   sister-in-law   uncle

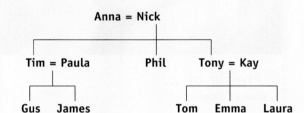

Anna = Nick

Tim = Paula   Phil   Tony = Kay

Gus   James   Tom   Emma   Laura

a) Tim is Paula's *husband*.

b) Gus is Laura's _____ .

c) Tony is James's _____ .

d) Tom is Phil's _____ .

e) Emma is Paula's _____ .

f) Kay is Phil's _____ .

g) Paula is Laura's _____ .

Pronunciation

1 Look at some words from Units 1–4. Say the words and add them to the table.

> ~~address~~ ~~assistant~~ Brazil Chinese computer ~~cousin~~ ~~hairdresser~~ husband lawyer manager Portugal umbrella

A: □□	B: □□□	C: □□	D: □□□
cousin	*hairdresser*	*address*	*assistant*

2 <u>Underline</u> the stressed syllable in each word.

🔊 1.58 Listen, check and repeat.

Reading & Listening

1 Read the text and answer the questions.

a) Who is the profile of?
b) Who is the writer of the profile?
c) What does Rona like?
d) What doesn't Rona like?

Meet my friend

Profile of ...
Rona Cameron

Sender: Kate Cameron

This is Rona. She's my best friend, and she's also my sister! She's fantastic, and she's single.
OK, what can I tell you about Rona? Well, she's thirty-one years old and she lives in Glasgow, in Scotland. She's a nurse, and she works at night, so she doesn't have a lot of time to meet new people. She likes eating out (her favourite food is Chinese), cooking, reading, listening to jazz and travelling. She speaks French, Italian and English. She loves football – it's her favourite sport. She watches football every weekend. She doesn't like shopping and loud music. She doesn't smoke.

Rona works hard but she also likes relaxing. She's a good friend and a great sister.

Contact Rona

2 Read the text again. Are the sentences true or false?

a) Kate is Rona's cousin. *False.*
b) Rona isn't married.
c) Rona is a waitress.
d) Rona meets a lot of new people.
e) Rona speaks three languages.
f) Rona's sister doesn't think Rona works hard.

3 🌐 1.59 Listen to a conversation between Rona and Kate. Which man does Rona call?

4 Listen again and complete the information about the three men.

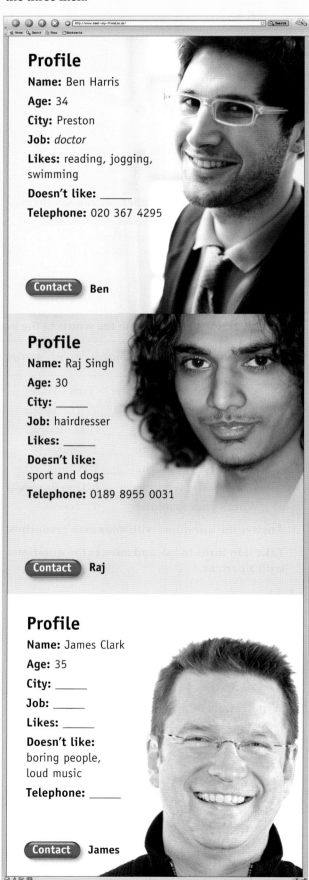

Profile

Name: Ben Harris

Age: 34

City: Preston

Job: *doctor*

Likes: reading, jogging, swimming

Doesn't like: _____

Telephone: 020 367 4295

Contact Ben

Profile

Name: Raj Singh

Age: 30

City: _____

Job: hairdresser

Likes: _____

Doesn't like: sport and dogs

Telephone: 0189 8955 0031

Contact Raj

Profile

Name: James Clark

Age: 35

City: _____

Job: _____

Likes: _____

Doesn't like: boring people, loud music

Telephone: _____

Contact James

Writing & Speaking

1 Match the punctuation features (*a–e*) with their names in the box.

> an apostrophe   a capital letter   a comma
> a full stop   a question mark

a) **.**   b) **,**   c) **?**   d) **'**   e) **A**

2 Complete the sentences with the names in Exercise 1.

a) You use *a question mark* at the end of a question.

b) You use _____ at the end of a sentence.

c) You use _____ to start a sentence and when you write names.

d) You use _____ to separate items in a list.

e) You use _____ for contractions or for possession.

3 Write questions with the question words in the box. Remember to start your questions with a capital letter and to use a question mark at the end of your questions.

> what   what's   where   who's

a) your / name? *What's your name?*
b) you / live
c) your / job
d) languages / speak
e) things / you / like
f) your / favourite singer
g) your / favourite food

4 Ask your partner the questions in Exercise 3. Complete the form with your partner's information.

> Where do you live?

> In Buenos Aires.

http://www.meet-my-friend.co.uk/

Profile

Name: _____

City: _____

Job: _____

Speaks: _____

Likes: _____

Favourite singer: _____

Favourite food: _____

Contact

5 Write about your partner using the information in their profile in Exercise 4.

Then exchange texts with your partner.

Check your partner's punctuation.

This is my friend, Marco Lupiano. He lives in Buenos Aires.

🔊 **1.60 Song:** *I Like The Way …*

5 Days

Grammar Present simple: daily routine. Telling the time
Vocabulary Days of the week. Verb phrases: *have* and *go*
Useful phrases Ordering and paying

Reading

1 🌐 1.61 **Listen and repeat the times. Then answer the questions.**

> 6.00 p.m.   6.30 a.m.   7.45 a.m.   11.00 p.m.
> 12.30 p.m.

a) Which times are before midday?
b) Which times are after midday?

2 **Read and complete the article with the times in Exercise 1.**

Seven perfect daily moments

According to British body-clock experts, these are the perfect times for routine activities.

Get up at (1) *6.30 a.m.* Your body wakes up with the sun.

Have breakfast at (2) _____ . Don't forget breakfast. It's a very important meal.

Do exercise at 8.15 a.m. You have a lot of energy in the morning.

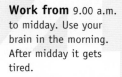

Work from 9.00 a.m. to midday. Use your brain in the morning. After midday it gets tired.

Have lunch at (3) _____ . Don't eat a big lunch. A sandwich is perfect.

Have dinner at (4) _____ . This is your big meal of the day. But don't eat late – your body needs time to digest before you go to bed.

Go to bed at (5) _____ . Your body likes seven or eight hours' sleep, so don't watch TV until midnight!

🌐 1.62 **Listen and check.**

3 **Tick (✓) if you agree with the times and explanations in the article. Put a cross (✗) if you don't agree.**

Compare with a partner.

Grammar

The time

What time is it?

It's twelve o'clock.

It's quarter past twelve.

It's half past twelve.

It's quarter to one.

12.00 a.m. = midnight

12.00 p.m. = midday

1 Match the times below with the times in the article on page 32.

a) nine o'clock in the morning *9.00 a.m.*
b) six o'clock in the evening
c) eleven o'clock at night
d) half past six in the morning
e) quarter to eight in the morning
f) quarter past eight in the morning

🔘 **1.63 Listen, check and repeat.**

2 What time is it? Write two ways of telling the time.

a) **2:30** It's two thirty. / *It's half past two.*
b) **7:15** It's _____ . / It's quarter past seven.
c) **1:10** It's one ten. / _____ .
d) **3:45** _____ . / It's quarter to four.
e) **4:55** It's four fifty-five. / _____ .
f) **9:40** It's nine forty. / _____ .

🔘 **1.64 Listen, check and repeat.**

3 Pairwork **Student A:** page 117 **Student B:** page 122

4 Ask your partner about what time they do routine activities. Use the verb phrases in the article on page 32.

> What time do you get up?

> At quarter to seven.

5 Grammar *Extra* 5 page 128. Read the explanation and do the exercises.

Pronunciation

1 🔘 1.65 Listen and repeat the long vowel sounds and examples.

/iː/	/ɜː/	/ɔː/
three	early	four
evening	birthday	morning

2 🔘 1.66 Listen and practise the sentences.

a) Don't eat three meals in the evening.
b) Stop work early: it's your birthday and you're thirty!
c) Don't call Paul before four in the morning.

Vocabulary

1 Complete the days of the week with the shortened forms in the box.

> Fri ~~Mon~~ Sat Sun Thu Tue Wed

(1) *Mon*day   (2) _____sday   (3) _____nesday   (4) _____rsday
(5) _____day   (6) _____urday   (7) _____day

2 🔘 1.67 Listen, check and repeat. What day is it today?

Listening

1 In your opinion, when do Tanya, Bill and Mary do each of the activities below?

a) Write *Sat* if you think it's on Saturday night.

b) Write *Sun* if you think it's on Sunday morning.

Tanya
- go out with friends
- go dancing
- drink cocktails
- have a good time
- read magazines

Bill
- go to work
- listen to the radio
- go home
- have a shower
- go to bed

Mary
- stay in
- have dinner
- watch television
- go on the internet
- go shopping

🔊 **1.68** Listen and check your ideas.

2 Tick (✓) the activities that you do at the weekend. Which day do you do them on? Compare with a partner.

Vocabulary & Speaking

1 Complete the verb phrases with *have* or *go*.

a) _____
- home
- on the internet
- out
- shopping
- to bed
- to work

b) _____
- a good time
- a shower
- breakfast
- dinner
- lunch

🔊 **1.69** Listen, check and repeat.

2 How is your weekend routine different from your weekday routine? Write notes.

At the weekend (Sat–Sun)	On weekdays (Mon–Fri)
I get up late.	I get up early.
I read the newspaper.	I don't read the newspaper.
I have lunch at home.	I have lunch at work.

Tell your partner about your weekend and weekday routines.

Reading

1 Look at Ms Dynamite's perfect weekend. Complete the text with the correct information.

Ms Dynamite's
perfect weekend

Saturday night
DVD: *Friends*
Restaurant: Blue Elephant
Food: Thai
Club: Attica
Drink: Vodka and Red Bull
Clothes: Armani or D&G

Sunday morning
Breakfast: Egg and bacon
Newspaper: *The Observer*
Book: *Rich Dad, Poor Dad* by Robert T Kiyosaki
TV: Soaps
CD: Billie Holiday
Clothes: Jeans

On Saturday night, she watches a (1) *DVD* or goes out with her friends. She goes to her favourite (2) _____ , the Blue Elephant, and has Thai food. She goes dancing at a (3) _____ called Attica. She drinks (4)_____ and Red Bull and she wears Armani or Dolce & Gabbana.

On Sunday morning, she has egg and bacon for (5) _____ . She reads the newspaper or a (6) _____ . Later, she watches soaps on (7) _____ or listens to CDs. On Sunday, she wears (8) ____ .

🔵 **1.70 Listen and check.**

2 Change the information in Exercise 1 to make it a perfect weekend for you.

Saturday night
DVD: A film with George Clooney
RESTAURANT: La Luna Caprese

Sunday morning
BREAKFAST: Black coffee

Writing

1 Write a paragraph about your perfect weekend. Use the information from Exercise 2 above.

On Saturday night, I watch a DVD or I go out with ...

2 Read about your partner's perfect weekend. Are you the same or different?

Useful phrases

1 🌐 **1.71 Read and listen to the conversations (a–d) and match them with the pictures (1–4).**

a) A: How much is it to the airport?
    B: £40.
    A: £40?! ... £20.
    B: OK, OK – £30.
    A: OK. Can I have a receipt, please?

b) C: How much is a bottle of champagne?
    D: £80, madam.
    C: Can I have two beers, please?

c) E: Can I have two tickets, please?
    F: How old are you?
    E: Er, 19.
    F: Can I see your ID?
    E: ID?
    F: Identity card.
    E: Oh.

d) G: Can I have the bill, please?
       ... Excuse me!
       Can I have the bill, please?
       ... THE BILL!
    H: The bill, sir?
    G: Yes, thank you.

2 Complete the useful phrases from the conversations in Exercise 1.

a) *How much is it* to the airport?

b) _____ a receipt, please?

c) _____ a bottle of champagne?

d) _____ two beers, please?

e) _____ two tickets, please?

f) _____ the bill, please?

🌐 **1.72 Listen, check and repeat.**

3 Work with a partner. Write a short conversation for each of these situations.

a) You want to order a bottle of wine.

b) You want to buy three tickets to a film with an 18 certificate at the cinema.

c) You want to take a taxi to the train station.

Practise the conversations.

Vocabulary *Extra*

Daily routine

1 Match the pictures with the verb phrases.

- [11] do <u>e</u>xercise
- [ ] <u>fi</u>nish work
- [ ] get up
- [ ] go home
- [ ] go on the <u>internet</u>
- [ ] go s<u>h</u>opping
- [ ] go to bed
- [ ] go to work
- [ ] have a <u>shower</u>
- [ ] have <u>break</u>fast
- [ ] have <u>d</u>inner
- [ ] have lunch
- [ ] <u>listen to music</u>
- [ ] read the <u>news</u>paper
- [ ] wake up

2 Tick (✓) the things in Exercise 1 that you do. Add three more things that you do in your daily routine.

3 When do you do these things?

<u>Morning</u>	*wake up*
Afternoon	
Evening	
Night	

Focus on *have*

1 Complete the table with the phrases in the box.

> have a BMW   ~~have dinner~~   have a good time   have lunch   have a meal   have a shower

Some uses of *have*	Examples
a) *have* = eat or drink	have a drink have a sandwich (1) *have dinner* (2) _____ (3) _____
b) *have* = do an activity	have a party have a game of tennis (4) _____
c) *have* = own or possess*	have three children have a Rolex watch have a small house (5) _____
d) expressions with *have*	have a nice day (6) _____

***Note:** When *have* means to own or possess you can also use *have/has got*.
I've got three children. *He's got* a Rolex watch. *We've got* a small house.

2 Write your own example sentences for each use of *have*.

6 Living

Grammar Present simple with adverbs of frequency. Prepositions of time
Vocabulary Verb phrases: *make* and *do*. Months. Ordinal numbers. Dates
Useful phrases Asking about opening and closing times

Reading

1 Look at the photographs and read the sentences. Guess which person the sentences describe. <u>Underline</u> *He* for Asashoryu or *She* for Jodie Kidd.

a) **He / She** lives in the country.
b) **He / She** doesn't have breakfast.
c) **He / She** listens to reggae in the morning.
d) **He / She** drinks a lot of water.
e) **He / She** trains for two hours every morning.
f) **He / She** has meat, fish and vegetables for lunch.
g) **He / She** does the housework at three o'clock in the afternoon.
h) **He / She** drives a Maserati.
i) **He / She** loves roast dinners and chocolate.

🌐 **1.73 Read the article. Check your answers about Jodie Kidd and Asashoryu.**

LITTLE and
LARGE

Jodie Kidd is a famous international model and a Maserati racing driver. She doesn't like cities. She lives in the country with her horses, dogs, cats and chickens. She hardly ever goes to the gym, but she really likes sports, especially polo and golf.
5   She also goes riding every day. She doesn't smoke and she doesn't usually drink alcohol. But she loves roast dinners and chocolate. She often visits her parents in their home in Barbados.

Asashoryu weighs 140 kilogrammes and is a grand champion of sumo wrestling. He lives at the Takasago 'stable' in Tokyo with thirty other
10 wrestlers. 'I always wake up before 7.00 a.m., make my bed and listen to reggae. I never have breakfast. I train for two hours. Then I have a shower. After training, I always drink a lot of water. For lunch I have meat, fish and vegetables. In the afternoon I sometimes have a nap or I sometimes go for a walk. At three o'clock in the afternoon we do the housework. In the evening I usually go out for a Chinese
15 meal or sushi. I'm always home at 11.30 p.m.'

2 Work with a partner. Make questions from the sentences in Exercise 1.

> Cibele, do you live in the country?

> No, I don't.

Write about your partner's answers.

Cibele doesn't live in the country.

Vocabulary

1 Complete the verb phrases with *make* or *do*.

a) _____
- (my) homework
- the housework
- the shopping
- the washing
- the washing up

b) _____
- a lot of noise
- dinner
- long phone calls
- the beds
- the decisions

🌐 **1.74 Listen, check and repeat.**

2 At home, who does or makes the things in Exercise 1? Make sentences and compare with your partner.

> My sister does her homework.

> My brother makes a lot of noise.

Grammar

Adverbs of frequency

Adverbs go before main verbs.
She **hardly ever** goes out.
He doesn't **usually** drink.
Do you **ever** walk to work?

Adverbs go after *be*.
I'm **always** at home.
He's **never** late.

1 Complete the chart with the adverbs of frequency highlighted in the article on page 38.

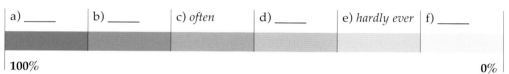

a) _____	b) _____	c) *often*	d) _____	e) *hardly ever*	f) _____

100%   **0%**

2 Add an adverb of frequency to make the sentences true for you.
a) I wake up before 7.00 a.m. *I hardly ever wake up before 7.00 a.m.*
b) I have a nap in the afternoon.
c) I visit my relatives at the weekend.
d) I'm at home in the evening.
e) I drink alcohol when I go out.
f) I'm late for work.

3 Find out your partner's answers. Ask questions with *Do you ever …?* or *Are you ever …?*

> Do you ever wake up before 7.00 a.m.?

> No, hardly ever.

4 Pairwork **Student A:** page 117 **Student B:** page 122

5 Grammar *Extra* 6 page 128. Read the explanation and do the exercises.

Pronunciation

Ordinal numbers

1st = first
2nd = second
3rd = third
4th = fourth
5th = fifth
6th = sixth
7th = seventh
8th = eighth
9th = ninth
10th = tenth

1 🌐 **1.75 Listen and repeat the ordinal words**

2 🌐 **1.76 Tick (✓) the group of ordinal numbers you hear.**

a) 1st 2nd 3rd ✓   3rd 2nd 1st ☐

b) 2nd 6th 7th ☐   7th 6th 2nd ☐

c) 4th 5th 1st ☐   5th 1st 4th ☐

d) 10th 12th 20th ☐   10th 20th 12th ☐

Vocabulary

1 Complete the months with a CAPITAL letter.

Spring	Summer	Autumn	Winter
March	__une	__eptember	__ecember
__pril	__uly	__ctober	__anuary
__ay	__ugust	__ovember	__ebruary

🌐 **1.77** Listen, check and repeat. Underline the stressed syllables.

Are the seasons the same months in your country?

2 Complete the table.

Dates	How to write dates	How to say dates
01/01	1$_{st}$ January	(1) *the first of January*
14/02	14$_{th}$ February	(2) _____
01/05	(3) _____	the first of May
31/10	31$_{st}$ October	(4) _____
25/12	(5) _____	the twenty-fifth of December

🌐 **1.78** Listen, check and repeat.

3 Work with a partner. Discuss the questions.
a) Which dates in the table are important in your country?
b) What other dates are important in your country?
c) What happens on these dates?

Grammar

Prepositions of time

in
the morning/afternoon/
evening
the spring/summer/
autumn/winter
January/February, etc.

on
Sunday/Monday, etc.
Friday night /
Sunday morning, etc.
1st May / 22nd June, etc.

at
night / the weekend
five o'clock / 2.45 p.m.,
etc.

1 Complete the sentences with *in*, *on* or *at*.
a) Something you never do *on* Sunday.
b) Something you always do _____ the morning.
c) Something you usually do _____ the weekend.
d) Something you always do _____ 31st December.
e) Something you sometimes do _____ Saturday night.
f) Something you usually do _____ the summer.

🌐 **1.79** Listen, check and repeat.

2 Write true sentences about the ideas in Exercise 1.

I never get up before 10.00 a.m. on Sunday.
I always drink tea in the morning.
I usually do the ironing at the weekend.

Compare your sentences with a partner.

Reading & Listening

1 🌐 **1.80 Read and match the festival information (*a–c*) with the photos (*1–3*).**

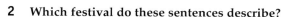

The top three world festivals

a) **The Oktoberfest** takes place in Munich, Germany. It starts on the third Saturday in September and goes on for two weeks. There are parades and people wear traditional clothes. Seven million visitors drink nine million litres of beer!

b) **San Fermín** takes place in Pamplona, Spain. It starts at midday on 6th July and goes on for one week. There's a bull-run every morning and parties all night. There are fireworks in the park and dancing in the streets. People drink sangria and have a great time.

c) **Rio Carnival** takes place in February or March in Rio de Janeiro, Brazil. It starts on a Saturday and ends on Tuesday (Mardi Gras). It goes on for four days. There's loud music, drumming and dancing. People wear colourful costumes and 70,000 people watch parades in the Sambadrome.

2 **Which festival do these sentences describe?**

a) People wear colourful costumes. *Rio Carnival*
b) People drink sangria.
c) There are fireworks in the park.
d) It takes place in February or March.
e) People wear traditional clothes.
f) It goes on for two weeks.

3 🌐 **1.81 Listen to a man and a woman talking about one of the festivals in Exercise 1 and answer the questions.**

a) Which festival is it?
b) Does the woman like it? Why? / Why not?
c) Does the man like it? Why? / Why not?

Which festival would you like to go to? Tell your partner.

Speaking: anecdote

1 🌐 **1.82 Listen to Conor talking about his favourite festival. <u>Underline</u> the correct information.**

a) 'What's the name of your favourite festival?' '<u>Saint Patrick's Day</u> / Halloween.'
b) 'When is it?' '**In March** / **In July.**'
c) 'How long does it go on for?' '**For a week** / **For four days.**'
d) 'What happens at the festival?' '**A parade and dancing** / **People give presents.**'
e) 'What do people wear?' '**Green clothes** / **Colourful costumes.**'
f) 'What do you drink?' '**Wine** / **Beer.**'
g) 'What kind of music do you listen to?' '**Traditional** / **Samba.**'

2 **You're going to tell your partner about your favourite festival or party.**

- Ask yourself the questions in Exercise 1.
- Think about *what* to say and *how* to say it.
- Tell your partner about your favourite festival or party.

My favourite festival is …

Useful phrases

1 🌐 1.83 **Read and listen to the conversations (a–c) and match them with pictures (1–3).**

---

a) Customer: Hello!
   Shop assistant: Sorry, we're closed.
   Customer: What time do you open?
   Shop assistant: We open at nine o'clock.
   Customer: But it's nine o'clock now.
   Shop assistant: No, it isn't. It's 8.57.

---

b) Anita: Oh no, we don't have any milk, and the supermarket's closed.
   Bob: The 7/11 is open.
   Anita: Oh, what time does it open?
   Bob: Seven o'clock.
   Anita: And what time does it close?
   Bob: Eleven o'clock.
   Anita: Ah yes. Seven-eleven!

---

c) Shop assistant: Good morning. Bling Jewellers.
   Customer: Oh hello. What time do you close, please?
   Shop assistant: We close at 5.30, madam.
   Customer: And what about on Sunday?
   Shop assistant: I'm sorry, we're closed on Sunday.
   Customer: Oh no – I work until six o'clock every day except Sunday.

2 **Write the useful phrases correctly with the words (in brackets).**

a) What time you open? (do) *What time do you open?*
b) We open nine o'clock. (at)
c) What time it open? (does)
d) What time it close? (does)
e) What time you close? (do)
f) We close 5.30. (at)
g) We're closed the weekend. (at)

🌐 1.84 **Listen, check and repeat the useful phrases.**

3 **Work with a partner. Practise the conversations in Exercise 1.**

4 **Work with a partner. Ask about opening and closing times in your city. Use the ideas in the box.**

---

the school   your bank   the local supermarket   your favourite bar   the post office

---

What time does the school open?   Nine o'clock.   And what time does it close?

Vocabulary *Extra*

Times of the year and dates

1 Match the pictures with the seasons.

☐ 3 autumn

☐ spring

☐ summer

☐ winter

2 Write the words or numbers.

1st = *first*

2nd = _____

3rd = _____

4th = _____

_____ = fifth

6th = _____

7th = _____

_____ = eighth

9th = _____

10th = _____

11th = _____

_____ = twelfth

13th = _____

14th = _____

15th = _____

_____ = sixteenth

_____ = seventeenth

18th = _____

19th = _____

_____ = twentieth

21st = _____

_____ = twenty-second

23rd = _____

24th = _____

25th = _____

_____ = twenty-sixth

27th = _____

28th = _____

29th = _____

_____ = thirtieth

31st = _____

3 Complete the months of the year.

Jan*uary*	July
Feb_____	Aug_____
Mar_____	Sept_____
Apr_____	Oct_____
May	Nov_____
June	Dec_____

4 Complete the days of the week.

Monday Tu_____ W_____ Th_____ F_____ Sa_____ Su_____

Focus on *go*

1 Complete the table with the phrases in the box.

go for a walk   go on the internet   go riding   go shopping   ~~go to bed~~   go to work

Some uses of *go*	Examples
a) *go to* + a place	go to Spain go to school go to the gym (1) *go to bed* (2) _____
b) *go* + *ing* = do an activity	go swimming go dancing (3) _____ (4) _____
c) *go* + *for a* + noun = do an activity	go for a drink go for a meal go for a ride (5) _____
d) verb phrases with *go*	go out every Saturday night go on holiday (6) _____

2 Write your own example sentences for each use of *go*.

7

Sea

Grammar Past simple: regular and irregular affirmative forms
Vocabulary Water sports. Time expressions. *ago*. Time linkers
Useful phrases Talking about the weather

Vocabulary & Listening

1 🌐 **2.01 Listen and repeat the names of the different water sports.**

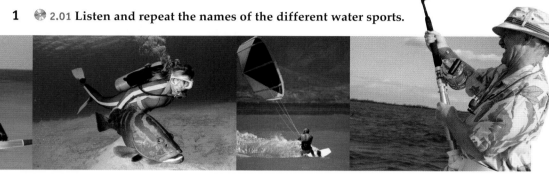

a) <u>wind</u>surfing
b) <u>scuba diving</u>
c) <u>kite surfing</u>
d) <u>fishing</u>

e) <u>surfing</u>
f) <u>sailing</u>
g) <u>swimming</u>

2 🌐 **2.02 Listen to two interviews about water sports. Circle the time expressions you hear in each interview.**

▲ Pam

▲ Sergio

	Pam	Sergio
went swimming	a) in 2006 / (in August)	c) on Monday / yesterday
went sailing	—	d) a long time ago / three days ago
went windsurfing	b) last week / last summer	—
went scuba diving	—	e) last year / last month

3 Complete the table to show two ways of saying the same thing.

on, in and *last*	*ago*
a) last week = *a week* ago	
b) on Saturday = _____ days ago	
c) last August = _____ month(s) ago	
d) in 2002 = _____ years ago	
e) in _____ = ten years ago	
f) on _____ = three days ago	

4 Which water sports do you like? Ask your partner.

Grammar

Past simple

	be	go
I	was	went
You	were	went
He	was	went
She	was	went
It	was	went
We	were	went
They	were	went

1 Rewrite two questions from the interview on page 44.

a) ever / you / go / Do / swimming ?

b) the last time/ was / When / went / you / swimming ?

🔘 **2.03 Listen, check and repeat.**

2 Ask your partner more questions about past activities. Use words and phrases in the box or your own ideas.

> dancing   shopping   skiing   to the beach   to the theatre   windsurfing

Do you ever go windsurfing?

Yes, I do.

When was the last time you went windsurfing?

Last summer.

Reading

1 🔘 **2.04 Read the article. What does the title mean (*a* or *b*)?**

a) Jack O'Neill always stays inside.

b) You are always warm in a wetsuit.

It's always warm on the inside

As a young man, Jack O'Neill worked for a big company, but he always went to the beach in his free time. He loved surfing, but the Californian ocean was cold. Jack wanted to find a way to stay warm in the water and he started to make protective clothing for cold water, or 'wetsuits'.

5 In 1952 he stopped working for the company and opened the first *Surf Shop*. He sold surfboards and wetsuits.

Jack demonstrated his wetsuits at boat exhibitions. He took his three young children with him. They wore wetsuits and sat in a bath of ice. When people asked, 'What's a wetsuit?' Jack pointed to his children.

10 O'Neill is a family-run company. There are seven children and they all work for the company. Jack lost his eye in a surfing accident, but he still surfs today.

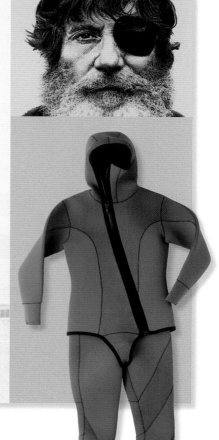

2 Complete the sentences about the article.

a) Jack O'Neill always went to the beach *in his free time*. (When?)

b) He surfed _____ . (Where?)

c) He started to make wetsuits _____ . (Why?)

d) He opened his first *Surf Shop* _____ . (When?)

e) At boat exhibitions his children wore wetsuits and sat _____ . (Where?)

f) He lost his eye _____ . (How?)

Grammar

Past simple

	Regular (work)	Irregular (have)
I	work**ed**	had
You	work**ed**	had
He	work**ed**	had
She	work**ed**	had
It	work**ed**	had
We	work**ed**	had
They	work**ed**	had

There is a list of irregular verbs on page 143.

1 Label the boxes *A* and *B*: *Regular verbs* or *Irregular verbs*.

> **A** _____
> call – called   like – liked
> play – played   stop – stopped
> study – studied   watch – watched

> **B** _____
> can – could   drive – drove
> fall – fell   make – made
> put – put   sit – sat

2 Match the sentence halves to make rules about forming regular past forms.

a) Most regular verbs (*watch*)   add *d* (*liked*)

b) Verbs ending in *e* (*like*)   add a consonant + *ed* (*stopped*)

c) Verbs ending in consonant + *y* (*study*)   add *ed* (*watched*)

d) Verbs ending in vowel + consonant (*stop*)   delete *y* and add *ied* (*studied*)

Write the past forms for these regular verbs: *ask, chat, finish, smile, start, try.*

3 Complete the verb groups with the irregular past forms in the box.

> broke   came   caught   ~~did~~   gave   heard   held   read   said   saw
> ~~sent~~   sold   spoke   thought   told   took   ~~went~~   wore

a) go – *went*   do – *did*   send – *sent*

b) hold – _____   sell – _____   tell – _____

c) think – _____   catch – _____   hear – _____

d) take – _____   break – _____   speak – _____

e) see – _____   come – _____   wear – _____

f) read – _____   say – _____   give – _____

🔘 2.05 **Listen, check and repeat.**

4 Practise saying the past forms of the verbs in Exercise 3. Circle the past form with the different sound in each group.

a)   *went* (*did*) *sent*

🔘 2.06 **Listen, check and repeat.**

5   Pairwork **Student A:** page 118   **Student B:** page 123

6   Grammar *Extra* 7 page 128. Read the explanation and do the exercises.

Pronunciation

1 Say the present and past forms of the verbs in the box. Which verbs have an extra syllable in the past form? Complete the table.

> ~~ask – asked~~   love – loved   ~~point – pointed~~   start – started   stop – stopped
> use – used   want – wanted   work – worked

A: No extra syllables	B: Extra syllable
☐ ➔ ☐	☐ ➔ ☐☐
ask – asked	*point pointed*

2   🔘 2.07 **Listen, check and repeat.**

Reading & Vocabulary

1 🌐 2.08 **Read the story about British actor, Richard E Grant. Are the following sentences true or false?**

a) Grant lived in Mozambique. *False*
b) Grant went fishing with his family.
c) There was a dolphin near the boat.
d) Grant fell in the water.
e) Grant's father became a hero.
f) Grant enjoyed the film *Jaws*.

Shark attack!

When he was eight, British actor, Richard E Grant went on holiday to Mozambique with his parents and his younger brother. One day, they went fishing in a small motor boat on an enormous lagoon called San Martina.

5 After an hour, the motor stopped, and they couldn't start it again. They shouted, but nobody heard them. Suddenly, something moved in the water near the boat.

At first, they thought it was a dolphin. But then they realised it was a big, grey shark. It started
10 knocking the boat. The boat rocked from side to side, and they nearly fell into the water. They were terrified. Grant's father tried to push the shark away, and his mother held him and his brother. They thought they were going to die.

15 Eventually, people in a fishing boat heard them and took them home. Everybody in the town heard about their story and talked about it. Grant's father became a local hero. Two or three weeks later, a local fisherman caught the shark and put it in the main square. Everybody came to
20 see the monster and took pictures of it.

Many years later, when Grant saw the film *Jaws*, he relived the terrible experience.

2 **Use the** highlighted **time linkers from the story about Richard E Grant to complete another story below.**

A man and woman went on holiday to the Indian Ocean. (1) *One day*, they went on a boat with twenty other people and went scuba diving. The boat stopped in the middle of the ocean, and everybody went diving.

(2) _____ , everybody returned to the boat, and the boat went back to the port. But the man and woman didn't return to the boat. When they finished diving, there was no boat. (3) _____ , they shouted, but nobody heard them. They waited and waited for the boat to return, but (4) _____ , they realised they were alone.

(5) _____ , something moved near them under the water.
(6) _____ , a fisherman found their camera.

🌐 2.09 **Listen and check.**

3 **In your opinion, what happened to the man and the woman?**

Useful phrases

1 🌐 **2.10 Read and listen to the conversations (a–c). Match the conversations with a sport in the box.**

fishing   jogging   sailing   skiing   swimming   windsurfing

Alan: Hello.
Mum: Hi, how are you?
Alan: Fine.
Mum: What's the weather like?
Alan: It's sunny and very windy.
Mum: Oh dear.
Alan: No – it's great. I want to go windsurfing. What's the weather like at home?
Mum: It's cloudy, it's raining and it's cold.
Alan: Oh dear.

Kim: Hello.
Dan: Hi, how are you?
Kim: Not very good.
Dan: Oh dear. Why?
Kim: It's sunny and warm. There isn't any snow.
Dan: Ah.
Kim: What's the weather like at home?
Dan: Um, it's snowing.
Kim: Oh!

Eric: Hello.
Jane: Hello. Did you catch any fish?
Eric: Er, no.
Jane: Where are you?
Eric: I'm not sure ... It's very foggy.

2 **Complete the table with words from the conversations in Exercise 1.**

Nouns		Useful phrases What's the (1) *weather* like?
☀	sun	It's (2) _____ .
🌳	wind	It's (3) _____ .
☁	cloud	It's (4) _____ .
🌧	rain	It's (5) _____ .
❄	snow	It's (6) _____ .
▦	fog	It's (7) _____ .

🌐 **2.11 Listen, check and repeat.**

3 **Work with a partner. Practise the conversations in Exercise 1.**

Vocabulary *Extra*

Sports

1 Match the pictures with the sports.

- 8 cycling
- ☐ fishing
- ☐ football
- ☐ jogging
- ☐ kite surfing
- ☐ riding
- ☐ sailing
- ☐ scuba diving
- ☐ surfing
- ☐ swimming
- ☐ tennis
- ☐ windsurfing

2 Work with a partner. Cover the words and look at the pictures. Ask and answer questions.

> What sport is number 1?

> Surfing.

Focus on *make* and *do*

1 Complete the table with the words in the box.

a decision   ~~dinner~~   exercise   my homework   a noise   the washing up

make and *do*	Examples
a) make …	coffee a mistake my bed a phone call (1) *dinner* (2) _____ (3) _____
b) do …	the shopping the housework the washing (4) _____ (5) _____ (6) _____

2 Write six of your own example sentences for these expressions with *make* and *do*.

8 Alone

Grammar Past simple: affirmative, negative and question forms
Vocabulary Feelings. Adjectives
Useful phrases Complaints and suggestions

Vocabulary

1 🔊 2.12 **Listen and repeat the adjectives in the box. Tick (✓) the words you know.**

> angry   bored   em<u>bar</u>rassed   ex<u>cit</u>ed   <u>fright</u>ened   <u>happy</u>   <u>ner</u>vous
> sad   <u>worried</u>

2 **Work with a partner. Look at the photographs (*a–f*). Find one or more adjectives from the box in Exercise 1 to describe the person's feelings in each photograph. Use your dictionary, if necessary.**

Speaking

1 **How do you feel in the different situations described in the box?**

> in a club or disco   in a fast car   in an exam   in a plane   now
> when you see a baby   when you see a spider   when you sing karaoke
> when you speak English

2 **Ask your partner.**

> How do you feel in an exam?

> Really nervous.

> Me too.

Reading & Writing

1 🌐 **2.13 Read the article and answer the questions.**

a) Who started the race? b) Who left the race? c) Who finished the race?

Alone **at sea**

Debra and Andrew Veal entered a 3,000-mile rowing race across the Atlantic from Tenerife to Barbados. There were thirty-four other rowing teams. They started the race together,
5 but after two weeks Andrew left the race because he was frightened of the ocean.

Debra didn't want to stop the race, and she decided to continue. She rowed the remaining 2,290 miles alone. The journey
10 took 113 days. Debra arrived in Barbados seventy days after the winning team, but for most people she was the hero of the race. The editor of *The Times* wrote, 'The winner of the race is the girl who came last.'

2 **Match the words in lists *A* and *B* to complete information from the article.**

A	B
a) a 3,000-mile	weeks
b) thirty-four	miles alone
c) two	rowing race
d) 2,290	days
e) 113	other rowing teams

3 **Cover the article and write sentences with the information in Exercise 2.**

a) Debra and Andrew Veal entered a 3,000-mile rowing race across the Atlantic.

Compare your sentences with a partner. Then compare your sentences with the text.

Listening & Vocabulary

1 🌐 **2.14 Listen to a radio programme about Debra Veal. Underline the correct information.**

a) Debra **was** / **wasn't** angry with her husband.
b) Debra **was** / **wasn't** worried about big ships.
c) Debra **was** / **wasn't** frightened of sharks.
d) The shark **was** / **wasn't** interested in Debra.
e) Debra **was** / **wasn't** embarrassed about coming last.
f) Debra **was** / **wasn't** happy about finishing the race.

2 **Complete the sentences with the prepositions in the box.**

about   about   in   of   with

a) I'm worried _____ my future.
b) I'm never angry _____ my friends.
c) I'm frightened _____ snakes.
d) I'm not interested _____ modern art.
e) I'm not embarrassed _____ my English.

🌐 **2.15 Listen, check and repeat.**

Tick (✓) the sentences that are true for you. Compare with your partner.

Reading

1 🔘 **2.16 Read about the life of Greta Garbo. How many times did she change her name?**

I WANT TO BE ALONE

Greta Garbo was a Hollywood star in the 1920s and 1930s. She was born in Sweden in 1906. Her real name was Greta Gustafsson. Her father died when she was fourteen, so she left school and got a job. She worked as a model for newspaper advertisements. When she was seventeen, she went to theatre
5 school.

She met Mauritz Stiller, a top Swedish film director, and he gave her a part in one of his films. He also gave her the name Garbo. In 1925, when Stiller moved to Hollywood, Garbo went with him. She later became an American citizen. In Hollywood, Garbo made twenty-seven films and got four Academy Award nominations. In 1932 in the film
10 *Grand Hotel* she said the famous line, 'I want to be alone.'

Garbo was not a typical Hollywood star. She was very private. She never spoke about her love affairs, and she didn't give interviews to the press. Many people fell in love with Garbo, and she had several serious relationships. But she never got married, and she didn't have any children.
15 When she was thirty-six, Garbo retired. She moved to New York, changed her name to Harriet Brown and lived the rest of her life there – alone. She died in 1990 at the age of eighty-four.

2 **Here is a summary of Greta Garbo's life. Put the lines in the correct order.**

   [1] a) Greta Garbo was born in Sweden. She left

   [   ] b) model. When she was seventeen, she went

   [   ] c) married and she didn't have

   [   ] d) thirty-six. She died in New York in 1990.

   [   ] e) to theatre school. Soon after, she moved to

   [2] f) school at fourteen and worked as a

   [   ] g) Hollywood and made twenty-seven films. She didn't get

   [   ] h) children. She retired when she was

🔘 **2.17 Listen and check.**

3 **Who is your favourite Hollywood star? What do you know about his or her life? Tell your partner about him or her.**

Writing

1 **Think about a retired person you know well. Write a summary of their life using the verb phrases in the box.**

- was born in … (a place, a year)
- went to … (school, university)
- left … (school, university)
- worked as a / an … (job)
- moved to … (a new place)
- lived in … (a place)

- met … (a person)
- got married to … (a person)
- got divorced from … (a person)
- had … children
- retired

2 **Compare your summary with a partner.**

Grammar

Past simple

I
You   **worked.**
He   **didn't work.**
She
It
We   **went.**
They   **didn't go.**

Did you work/go?
Yes, I **did.**
No, I **didn't.**

⚠ You don't use
did/didn't with *be*.

1 **Complete the questions and answers about your family's past.**

a) '*Did* you go to primary school near here?'   'Yes, *I did.*'   'No, *I didn't.*'
b) '*Did* you walk to school?'   'Yes, *I did.*'   'No, *I didn't.*'
c) '_____ you move house when you were a child?'   '_____.'   '_____.'
d) '_____ your father leave school at sixteen?'   '_____.'   '_____.'
e) '_____ your mother study English at school?'   '_____.'   '_____.'
f) '_____ your parents go to university?'   '_____.'   '_____.'

🌐 **2.18 Listen, check and repeat.**

2 **Work with a partner. Ask and answer the questions in Exercise 1.**

3 Pairwork **Student A:** page 118 **Student B:** page 123

4 Grammar *Extra* 8 page 128. Read the explanation and do the exercises.

Pronunciation

1 **Complete lists *A* and *B* with the past simple forms of the irregular verbs.**

A	B
feel *felt*	break
know	fly
mean	spell *spelt*
see	spend
speak	teach
think	wear

🌐 **2.19 Listen, check and repeat.**

2 **Match a verb from list *A* with a verb from list *B* according to the sound of the past simple form.**

🌐 **2.20 Listen, check and repeat.**

Speaking: anecdote

1 🌐 **2.21 Listen to Lottie talking about her last summer holiday. <u>Underline</u> the correct information.**

a) 'Where did you go?' 'I went **to the beach** / **to the mountains**.'
b) 'When did you go there?' 'I went **last month** / **in July**.'
c) 'Who did you go with?' 'I went **with my family** / **alone**.'
d) 'How did you get there?' 'I went **by train** / **by plane and by car**.'
e) 'Where did you stay?' 'I stayed **in a hotel** / **with friends**.'
f) 'How long did you stay?' 'I stayed for **two weeks** / **a month**.'
g) 'What did you do all day?' 'I **visited the area** / **went to the beach**.'
h) 'What did you do in the evening?' 'I **went out to the bars and clubs** / **went shopping**.'

2 **You are going to tell your partner about your last summer holiday.**

• Ask yourself the questions in Exercise 1.
• Think about *what* to say and *how* to say it.
• Tell your partner about your last summer holiday.

Last summer I went to ...

www.hotelhurricane.com

Useful phrases

1 🔊 **2.22 Read and listen to the conversations (a–d) and match them with the pictures (1–4).**

a)
  Nick: I'm thirsty.
  Gill: Me too – let's have a nice cup
          of tea.
  Nick: Tea? No, thanks. I'd like a beer!

b)
  Son: I'm bored.
  Mum: Why don't you read a book?
  Son: A book? No, thank you!

c)
  Alice: I'm hungry. Is it lunchtime?
  Brigit: No, it's half past eleven.
         Why don't you eat some fruit?
  Alice: No, thanks. Do you have any
         chocolate?

d)
  Derek: I'm tired.
  Sue: Me too. Let's stay at home
         tonight.
  Derek: Good idea. There's football
         on TV.

2 🔊 **2.23 Listen and repeat the useful phrases.**

a) I'm thirsty.
b) Let's have a nice cup of tea.
c) I'm bored.
d) Why don't you read a book?
e) I'm hungry.
f) I'm tired.
g) Me too.

3 **Complete these conversations with phrases from Exercise 2.**

a) '*I'm bored.*' 'Why don't you go out with your friends?'

b) '_____ .' 'Why don't you have a snack?'

c) '_____ .' 'Me too. Let's watch a DVD tonight.'

d) '_____ .' 'Why don't you have lunch early?'

e) '_____ .' 'Me too. Let's have a cup of coffee.'

f) '_____ .' 'Why don't you play on your PlayStation?'

🔊 **2.24 Listen, check and repeat.**

4 **Work with a partner. Write similar conversations to the ones in Exercise 1. Use the problems in the box or your own ideas.**

I'm cold.   I'm frightened of flying.   I'm hot.   I'm worried about my exams.

Practise your conversations.

Vocabulary *Extra*

Feelings

1 Match the pictures with the feelings.

- [4] She's <u>ang</u>ry
- [ ] She's bored
- [ ] He's em<u>bar</u>rassed
- [ ] They're ex<u>ci</u>ted
- [ ] He's <u>frigh</u>tened
- [ ] She's very <u>inter</u>ested
- [ ] She's sad
- [ ] He's <u>wor</u>ried

2 Match the sentence beginnings in Exercise 1 with the sentence endings below.

4 – f She's angry with her son.

- a) ... about his body.
- b) ... about the future.
- c) ... about their holiday.
- d) ... about going.
- e) ... in horses.
- f) ... with her son.
- g) ... of dogs.
- h) ... with her job.

Focus on the weather

1 Match the pictures with the words.

- [6] It's <u>cloud</u>y.
- [ ] It's cold.
- [ ] It's <u>fog</u>gy.
- [ ] It's hot.
- [ ] It's <u>rain</u>ing.
- [ ] It's <u>snow</u>ing.
- [ ] It's <u>sun</u>ny.
- [ ] It's <u>wind</u>y.

2 What's the weather like today?

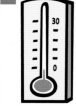

Review B

Grammar

► Grammar *Extra* pages 128 and 129

1 Complete the sentences with the present simple form of the verbs in the box.

> do   get up   go   have   live   ~~work~~

a) I *work* from 9.00 a.m. to 5.00 p.m.
b) My mother _____ to the supermarket on Fridays.
c) We _____ near the station.
d) Sue _____ exercise after work.
e) John and Ella _____ early in the morning.
f) Pete _____ breakfast at work.

Write sentences in the negative.

a) I don't work from 9.00 a.m. to 5.00 p.m.

2 Match the times.

a) It's 5.30.   1   It's quarter to five.
b) It's 10.15.   2   It's ten to seven.
c) It's 6.50.   3   It's midnight.
d) It's 11.10.   4   It's half past five.
e) It's 4.45.   5   It's ten past eleven.
f) It's 12.00 a.m.   6   It's quarter past ten.

3 Put the adverbs of frequency in order (*1–6*).

> ~~always~~   hardly ever   never   often
> sometimes   usually

100%					0%
1 *always*	2	3	4	5	6

4 Put the words in the correct order.

a) a nap / I / sometimes / at work / have
   I sometimes have a nap at work.
b) make / long phone calls / never / I
c) my bed / I / make / always
d) listen / hardly ever / I / to reggae
e) I / go / often / to the gym
f) usually / have / I / with my family / dinner

Change the sentences to make them true for you.

a) I never have a nap at work.

Compare with a partner.

5 Complete the table with the phrases in the box.

> ~~the evening~~   1997   Wednesday   8.15
> night   10th March   the summer   July
> Thursday morning   the morning
> eleven o'clock   the weekend

at	in	on
	the evening	

Which phrases in the box can come after *last*?

6 Complete the story. Use the verbs in the box in the past simple form.

> ~~ask~~   not be   go   have   jump   lose
> save   see   sit   think

Ron (1) *asked* Lulu to go out with him last Saturday. They (2) _____ lunch on the beach. Ron (3) _____ on Lulu's sunglasses! Lulu (4) _____ very happy.

In the afternoon Lulu (5) _____ swimming. Ron (6) _____ something in the water. He (7) _____ it was a shark! But it was only a dolphin.

Later, Ron (8) _____ into the water. He (9) _____ his glasses. A lifeguard (10) _____ him.

7 Make questions about Ron and Lulu's story.

a) When / Ron and Lulu / go to the beach?
   When did Ron and Lulu go to the beach?
b) Who / sit on Lulu's sunglasses?
c) What / Lulu do in the afternoon?
d) Who / see something in the water?
e) What / Ron lose?
f) Who / save Ron?

Work with a partner and answer the questions.

8 Spot the mistake! Cross out the incorrect sentence, *a* or *b*.

1 a) ~~It twelve o'clock.~~
   b) It's twelve o'clock.

2 a) He work with me.
   b) He works with me.

3 a) What time do you go to bed?
   b) What time you go to bed?

4 a) I saw that film last week.
   b) I saw that film the last week.

5 a) We go to town yesterday.
   b) We went to town yesterday.

6 a) Were you there on Monday?
   b) Did you were there on Monday?

Vocabulary

1 Write the days of the week.

a) The first day of the week. *Monday*
b) The seventh day of the week.
c) The day after Tuesday.
d) The fifth day of the week.
e) The second day of the week.
f) The day before Sunday.
g) The fourth day of the week.

2 Look at the pictures of Carmen's day. Label the pictures with *have* or *go* and the words in the box.

> ~~breakfast~~   to bed   dinner   a good time
> home   lunch   on the internet   shopping
> a shower   to work

a) *have breakfast*

3 Write the dates in words.

a) 6/01 *the sixth of January*
b) 22/02   e) 12/05   h) 24/08   k) 8/11
c) 15/03   f) 23/06   i) 20/09   l) 31/12
d) 5/04   g) 1/07   j) 17/10

4 Complete the phrases with *make* or *do*.

a) *do* the washing up
b) _____ a phone call
c) _____ the housework
d) _____ your homework
e) _____ dinner
f) _____ the shopping
g) _____ your bed
h) _____ the washing

Work with a partner. Ask questions with *When was the last time you made/did ...?*

a) *When was the last time you did the washing up?*

5 Complete the sentences with the adjectives in the box.

> angry   bored   embarrassed   excited
> frightened   ~~happy~~   nervous   sad   worried

a) I was very *happy* when I passed my driving test.
b) This film is too long. I'm really _____ !
c) Jim was _____ with Sue because she broke his camera.
d) It's my 21st birthday tomorrow. I'm so _____ !
e) Oh, help! I'm _____ of snakes!
f) Jo was _____ when she forgot her teacher's name.
g) Jan was very _____ when her cat died.
h) Is Ben OK? I'm very _____ about him.
i) I don't like exams. I get very _____ .

6 Complete the words for water sports with *a, e, i, o, u.*

a) f*i*shing
b) k__t__   s__rf__ng
c) s__ __l__ng
d) sc__b__   d__v__ng
e) s__rf__ng
f) sw__mm__ng
g) w__nds__rf__ng

Pronunciation

1 Look at some words from Units 5–8. Say the words and add them to the table.

> ~~August~~   breakfast   ~~embarrassed~~   excited
> ~~exercise~~   frightened   internet   nervous
> November   October   Saturday   September
> terrible   Thursday   usually

A: □□	B: □□□	C: □□□
August	*exercise*	*embarrassed*

2 Underline the stressed syllable in each word.

🔘 2.25 **Listen, check and repeat.**

Reading & Listening

1 **Work with a partner. Discuss the question.**

How do you spend your free time? Do you …
- play games? (sports, computer games)
- do creative things? (paint, write, make music)
- relax? (listen to music, read, watch DVDs)
- help people? (youth club, community work)

2 🌐 **2.26 Read the text and match photos *a–c* with photos *1–3*.**

▲ Angelina Jolie   ▲ Sean Penn   ◀ Bono

CELEBRITY
free time

These days some actors and singers want to do more than act and sing – they want to spend their free time helping other people.

Angelina Jolie does a lot of work for UNICEF (the United Nations Children's Fund). She travels to Africa, South-East Asia and South
5 America. She gives her time to children who need help. People all over the world watch her on TV, working with poor children. They feel sympathetic and send money to UNICEF.

Bono, singer in the rock band U2, also does a lot of work for charity. He started his work for charity in 1979 with a concert for Amnesty
10 International. In 2005 he helped to organise the Live 8 concerts. He asked the world's rich countries to give money to the world's poor countries.

After Hurricane Katrina in 2005, the city of New Orleans was under water. Many people died and many other people lost their homes. Actor
15 **Sean Penn** saw a news story on TV and went to New Orleans. He helped the frightened people and took them to hospital in his boat.

3 **Read the text again. Complete the sentences with information in the box.**

> 1979   boat   Live 8   New Orleans   time   ~~UNICEF~~

a) Angelina Jolie does a lot of work for *UNICEF* .
b) Angelina Jolie gives her _____ to children who need help.
c) Bono started doing charity work in _____ .
d) In 2005 Bono helped to organise _____ .
e) After Hurricane Katrina the city of _____ was under water.
f) Sean Penn saved people in his _____ .

4 🌐 **2.27 Listen to the news report about actor and writer David Walliams' charity swim. Complete the sentence.**

David swam from England to _____ .

5 **Listen again. <u>Underline</u> the correct information.**

a) Greg Whyte is David Walliams' **friend** / <u>**trainer**</u> / **cousin**.
b) David swam **14** / **24** / **34** kilometres.
c) His swim took **10 hours 30 minutes** / **12 hours 30 minutes** / **15 hours 30 minutes**.
d) He arrived in France at **4.00 p.m.** / **5.00 p.m.** / **6.00 p.m.**
e) After his swim he felt very **happy** / **sad** / **angry**.
f) He made more than **£10,000** / **£100,000** / **£1,000,000**.

Writing & Speaking

1 Read about a memorable day and match the questions (*a–f*) with the answers in note form (*1–6*).

A memorable day

My memorable day happened six years ago. I was in Fréjus, a small town in the south of
5 France. It was a beautiful, sunny day, and I went to a rock concert to see my favourite band. I only had one ticket, so I went
10 alone. The concert was great, and the other fans were really nice. Later that evening, I went to a club, and the band were there!
15 I spoke to them, and they gave me two free tickets for their next concert. I was so happy!

a) When was it?
b) Where were you?
c) What was the weather like?
d) Who were you with?
e) What did you do/see?
f) How did you feel at the end of the day?

1 Fréjus, France
2 spoke to my favourite band
3 six years ago
4 happy
5 went alone
6 sunny

2 Work with a partner. Read the notes and complete the story of another memorable day.

- near Rome, Italy
- won a dancing competition
- two years ago
- tired
- my boyfriend
- sunny

My memorable day happened (1) *two years ago*. I was in a small town near (2) _____ , in (3) _____ . It was a hot, (4) _____ day. I was with (5) _____ . We entered a (6) _____ and we (7) _____ first prize. At the end of the day we were very (8) _____ , but it was a fantastic day.

3 Think of a memorable day in your life. Answer the questions in note form.
a) When was it?
b) Where were you?
c) What was the weather like?
d) Who were you with?
e) What did you do/see?
f) How did you feel at the end of the day?

4 From your notes, write a full story of a memorable day in your life.

🎵 **2.28 Song:** *Don't Worry, Be Happy*

9 Hotel

Grammar *there is / there are. some/any*
Vocabulary Rooms and furniture. Prepositions of place
Useful phrases Problems with a hotel room

Reading & Listening

1 **Look at the photos and complete the text with** *Little Palm Island* **or** *Emirates Palace Hotel.*

▼ Little Palm Island

▼ Emirates Palace Hotel

For the holiday of a lifetime

Choose the peace of **Little Palm Island**, or the luxury of the **Emirates Palace Hotel**

(1) _____ is the perfect place to relax and escape the stress of work and family life. The tropical island is just 120 miles from Miami International Airport. There are thirty suites. The rooms are simple and spacious. You can relax on the veranda, or visit the beautiful spa. It's paradise. A Grand Suite costs $2,000 for one night.

(2) _____ cost $3 billion to build. There are four restaurants, three bars, two fitness centres and two swimming pools. The rooms are enormous, and the public living room is 175 metres long. There are 302 luxury rooms and 44 suites. Every room is beautiful and has the latest technology. A luxury suite costs $3,000 for one night.

🔊 **2.29 Listen and check.**

2 **Work with a partner. Read the sentences. Write** *E* **if you think the sentence describes the** *Emirates Palace Hotel.* **Write** *L* **if you think the sentence describes** *Little Palm Island.*
   a) There isn't a road to the hotel: guests arrive by boat or seaplane. *L*
   b) There are 2,600 employees – that's four for every guest in the hotel.
   c) There are 1,000 crystal chandeliers.
   d) There aren't any phones or TVs.
   e) There's a 125-centimetre plasma TV in every room.
   f) There aren't any children – sixteen is the minimum age.

🔊 **2.30 Listen and check.**

Which hotel do you prefer?

3 **What's the name of your favourite hotel? Tell your partner about it.**

Vocabulary

1 Work with a partner. Match the pictures with the words.

> an <u>arm</u>chair   a bath   a <u>book</u>case   a <u>car</u>pet   a <u>cof</u>fee table   a <u>cook</u>er
> a <u>cup</u>board   <u>cur</u>tains   <u>cush</u>ions   a desk   a fridge   a lamp   a <u>mir</u>ror
> plants   a rug   a <u>show</u>er   a <u>so</u>fa   a <u>wash</u>basin

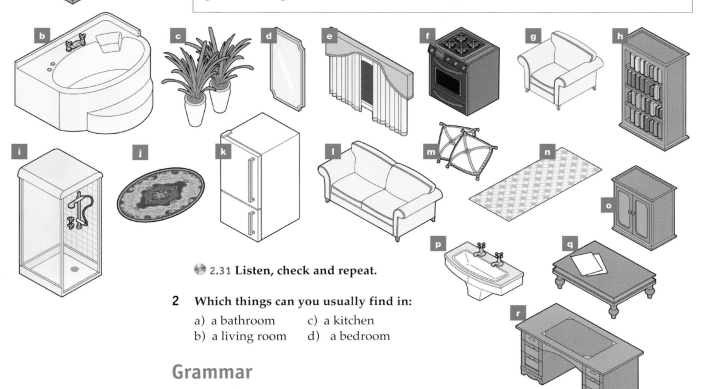

🔘 2.31 Listen, check and repeat.

2 Which things can you usually find in:

a) a bathroom   c) a kitchen
b) a living room   d) a bedroom

Grammar

there is / there are some/any

Singular
There's **a** carpet
There isn't **a** rug.

Plural
There are **some** cushions.
There aren't **any** plants.

1 Look at the photo. In your opinion, is this bedroom on *Little Palm Island* or in the *Emirates Palace Hotel*?

2 Complete the sentences about the hotel bedroom with the words in the box.

> ~~bed~~   clocks   bookcase   curtains

a) There's a *bed*.   c) There are some _____ .
b) There isn't a _____ .   d) There aren't any _____ .

🔘 2.32 Listen, check and repeat.

3 Write similar sentences about the hotel room using the sentence beginnings in Exercise 2.

There's a sofa. There are some lamps.

Vocabulary

1 **Look at the photo and complete the sentences.**

a) There's a rug *on the floor.*

b) There's a lamp …

c) There's a magazine …

d) There's a plant …

e) There are some cushions …

f) There are some pictures …

> in the corner.
> next to the sofa.
> ~~on the floor.~~
> on the sofa.
> on the wall, above the sofa.
> under the coffee table.

🔊 2.33 **Listen, check and repeat.**

2 **Describe the location of the things in Exercise 1 in your home.**

> There's a lamp on the table next to my bed in my bedroom.

Grammar

Is/Are there …?

Singular

Is there a mirror?
Yes, **there is.**
No, **there isn't.**

Plural

Are there any plants?
Yes, **there are.**
No, **there aren't.**

1 **Complete the questions and answers.**

a) '*Is* there a computer in your living room?'   'Yes, *there is.*'   'No, *there isn't.*'

b) '*Are* there any plants in your kitchen?'   'Yes, *there are.*' 'No, _____ .'

c) '_____ there _____ pictures in your bedroom?'   '_____ .' '_____ .'

d) '_____ there _____ carpet in your bathroom?'   '_____ .' '_____ .'

e) '_____ there _____ television in your bathroom?'   '_____ .' '_____ .'

f) '_____ there _____ cushions in your bedroom?'   '_____ .' '_____ .'

🔊 2.34 **Listen, check and repeat.**

2 **Work with a partner. Ask and answer the questions in Exercise 1.**

3 Grammar *Extra 9* page 130. Read the explanation and do the exercises.

4 Pairwork **Student A:** page 118 **Student B:** page 123

Pronunciation

1 🔊 2.35 **Listen and repeat the words in the box. Do you pronounce the consonants in red?**

> au<u>t</u>umn /'ɔːtəm/   cup<u>b</u>oard /'kʌbəd/   eigh<u>t</u> /eɪt/   i<u>s</u>land /'aɪlənd/   <u>k</u>now /nəʊ/
>
> lis<u>t</u>en /'lɪsn/   re<u>c</u>eipt /rɪˈsiːt/   <u>w</u>rite /raɪt/

2 **Practise the words.**

in the city

on a hill

near the sea

Vocabulary

1   Circle the correct prepositions.

a)   I live **in** / **on** the city.

b)   I live **in** / **on** a hill.

c)   I live **in** / **near** the sea.

d)   I live **in** / **on** the mountains.

e)   I live **in** / **on** the country.

f)   I live **in** / **on** an island.

g)   I live **in** / **near** a river.

h)   I live **in** / **on** a small village.

i)   I live **in** / **on** the coast.

j)   I live **near** / **on** the top floor.

k)   I live **in** / **near** a lake.

l)   I live **near** / **on** a park.

🔘 **2.36 Listen, check and repeat.**

2   Write three sentences about where you live, using the prepositions in Exercise 1.

I live in the city. I live near a park …

Reading

1   Complete the horoscope with the correct prepositions (*in, on, near*).

Your home in the stars

Do you know where you want to live? Apparently, it all depends on your star sign.

CAPRICORN
22nd Dec – 19th Jan
You want to live in a small village (1) *in* the mountains.

AQUARIUS
20th Jan – 17th Feb
You want to live in a big, spacious house (2) _____ a hill.

PISCES
18th Feb – 19th Mar
You're happy when you're (3) _____ the sea.

ARIES
20th Mar – 19th Apr
You love living in the city because you want to be (4) _____ the shops.

TAURUS
20th Apr – 20th May
You want two homes: a flat (5) _____ the city and a weekend house in a small village.

GEMINI
21st May – 20th June
You can't decide! You like living in the city, but you also like being in the country or (6) _____ the coast.

CANCER
21st June – 22nd July
You love water – you want a house (7) _____ a lake or a river.

LEO
23rd July – 22nd Aug
You want to live in a big house (8) _____ a hot country.

VIRGO
23rd Aug – 22nd Sep
You want to live (9) _____ the top floor of a block of flats in the city centre.

LIBRA
23rd Sep – 22nd Oct
You want a beautiful house near a lake (10) _____ the country.

SCORPIO
23rd Oct – 21st Nov
You want to live (11) _____ a tropical island.

SAGITTARIUS
22nd Nov – 21st Dec
You like the city and the country, so you want to live in the city (12) _____ a big park.

🔘 **2.37 Listen and check.**

2   Work in small groups. Discuss the questions.

a)   Do you agree with the description for your star sign?

b)   Which is the best description for you?

Useful phrases

1 🔊 **2.38 Read and listen to the three conversations between a hotel receptionist (R) and a hotel guest (G). What problems are there with the hotel room?**

R: Reception. Can I help you?
G: Yes, this is room 45. I have a problem with the television.
R: Oh dear, I'm sorry to hear that, sir. What's the problem?
G: It doesn't work.
R: Oh, I'm sorry, sir. I'll send someone immediately.

R: Reception. Can I help you?
G: This is room 45. I have a problem with the bathroom.
R: Oh, I'm sorry, sir. What's the problem?
G: There aren't any towels.
R: Oh, I'm sorry, sir. I'll send someone immediately.

R: Hello, sir.
G: Room 45. I have another problem.
R: Oh dear. What's the problem now, sir?
G: The shower doesn't work.
R: Oh, I'm sorry, sir. There's a bath in your room.
G: There isn't any hot water for a bath.
R: Oh, right. Would you like a different room, sir?
G: No, I'd like a different hotel.

2 🔊 **2.39 Listen and repeat the useful phrases.**

a) Can I help you?
b) I have a problem with the television.
c) What's the problem?
d) It doesn't work.
e) The shower doesn't work.

Practise the conversations in Exercise 1 with a partner.

3 Work with a partner. Write similar conversations. Use the problems in the box or your own ideas.

> The alarm clock / hairdryer / heating / light doesn't work.
> There isn't a remote control for the TV.
> There isn't any soap / shampoo.

Practise your conversations.

Vocabulary *Extra*

In a house

1 Match the pictures with the things in the house.

- [23] an <u>ar</u>mchair
- [ ] a bath
- [ ] a bed
- [ ] a <u>book</u>case
- [ ] a <u>car</u>pet
- [ ] a clock
- [ ] a <u>coffee ta</u>ble
- [ ] a <u>coo</u>ker
- [ ] a <u>cup</u>board
- [ ] <u>cur</u>tains
- [ ] a <u>cush</u>ion
- [ ] a desk
- [ ] a floor
- [ ] a fridge
- [ ] a lamp
- [ ] a <u>mir</u>ror
- [ ] a <u>pic</u>ture
- [ ] a plant
- [ ] a rug
- [ ] a <u>show</u>er
- [ ] a <u>so</u>fa
- [ ] a wall
- [ ] a <u>wash</u>basin

What are the names of the four rooms?

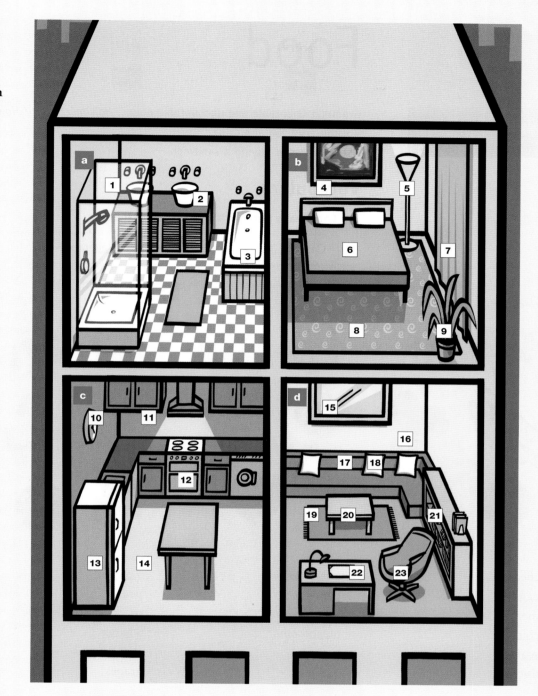

2 Work with a partner. Cover the words and look at the picture.
Ask and answer questions.

> What's this?

> A bed.

> What are these?

> Curtains.

Focus on prepositions of place (1)

1 Complete the table with the phrases in the box.

> the country   an island
> a park   the shops
> the top floor   ~~a village~~

Prepositions	Examples
in …	the city the mountains (1) *a village* (2) _____
on …	a hill the coast (3) _____ (4) _____
near …	the sea a river a lake (5) _____ (6) _____

2 Where would you like to live? Use the phrases in Exercise 1.

10 Food

Grammar Countable and uncountable nouns. *How much ...? / How many ...?*
Vocabulary Food and drink
Useful phrases Buying a sandwich

Vocabulary

1 Label each photo with a word from the box.

Carbohydrates   Fruit   Proteins   Vegetables

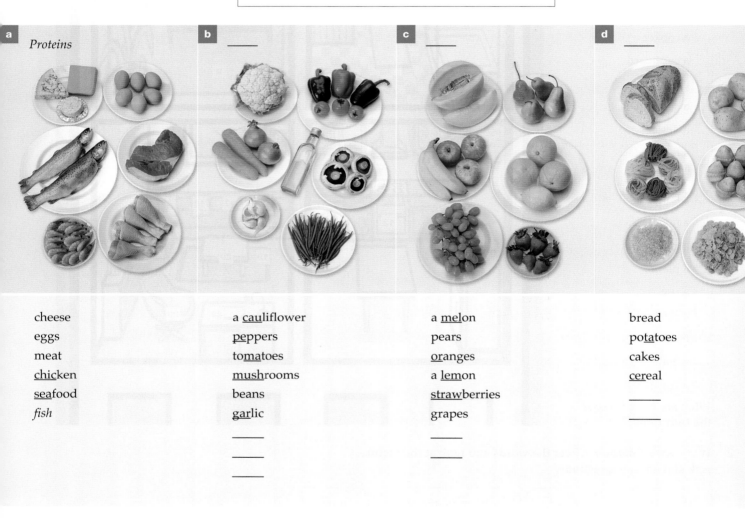

a Proteins

cheese
eggs
meat
chicken
seafood
fish

b _____

a cauliflower
peppers
tomatoes
mushrooms
beans
garlic
_____
_____
_____

c _____

a melon
pears
oranges
a lemon
strawberries
grapes
_____
_____

d _____

bread
potatoes
cakes
cereal
_____
_____

2 Complete the lists in Exercise 1 with the words in the box.

apples   bananas   carrots   fish   olive oil   onions   pasta   rice

🌐 **2.40** Listen, check and repeat the lists.

3 Look at the food lists again. Write down:
   a) food you often eat.
   b) food you sometimes eat.
   c) food you never or hardly ever eat.

Compare your answers with your partner.

Pronunciation

🔊 **2.41 Listen and repeat the words. In each group, circle the word with the different vowel sound.**

a) meat (bread) beans   c) potato tomato banana

b) apple carrot garlic   d) pepper cereal melon

🔊 **2.42 Listen, check and repeat.**

Grammar

Countable and uncountable nouns

Countable: singular
a melon
a grape

Countable: plural
two melons
some grapes

Uncountable
some milk (NOT ~~one milk~~)
some pasta (NOT ~~three pastas~~)

1 Complete the table with food from the photos on page 66.

Nouns you can count		Nouns you can't count
singular countable	**plural countable**	**uncountable**
There's a *cauliflower*.	There are some _____ .	There's some _____ .
There's a _____ .	There are some _____ .	There's some _____ .
There's a _____ .	There are some _____ .	There's some _____ .

2 Complete the questions and answers about the food photos on page 66.

a) '*Are* there any mushrooms in photo *b*?' 'Yes, *there are.*' 'No, *there aren't*.'

b) '*Is* there any cheese in photo *c*?' 'Yes, *there is.*' 'No, _____ .'

c) '_____ there a cauliflower in photo *b*?' '_____ .' '_____ .'

d) '_____ there any pasta in photo *d*?' '_____ .' '_____ .'

e) '_____ there any bananas in photo *d*?' '_____ .' '_____ .'

f) '_____ there any bread in photo *a*?' '_____ .' '_____ .'

🔊 **2.43 Listen, check and repeat.**

3 Work with a partner. Ask and answer the questions in Exercise 2.

Ask more questions. Use other food words from page 66.

> Are there any potatoes in photo *d*?

> Yes, there are. Is there any rice in photo *a*?

> No, there isn't.

Speaking

1 Write a shopping list with your six favourite food items from the food photos on page 66.

2 Try to guess which six items are on your partner's shopping list.

Ask questions to check.

> Are there any strawberries?

> No, there aren't.

Shopping list

onions
potatoes
eggs

Reading & Listening

1 🌐 **2.44 Read the article and complete the sentences.**

a) Don't eat _____ with proteins.

b) Don't eat _____ with other food.

c) Eat _____ with any kind of protein or carbohydrate.

Eat well, enjoy your food and lose weight

Imagine a diet where you can eat three meals a day and lose weight! With 'food-combining', you can eat what you like, but there are some things you can't eat together.

5   'Food-combining' is based on the way we digest food. The human body digests different food in different ways. Fruit only takes half an hour to digest, but carbohydrates take three to four hours, and proteins take up to eight

10 hours. This is why it is important to eat the same kinds of food together. You just need to follow three simple rules.

1 The fruit rule
Don't eat fruit with other food.

2 The protein and carbohydrate rule
Don't eat proteins and carbohydrates at the same meal.

3 The vegetable rule
Eat vegetables (or salads) with any kind of protein or carbohydrate.

2 **According to the rules in the article, which meal will help you lose weight?**

a) Steak and chips.

b) Fish and rice.

c) Fish and vegetables.

d) Spaghetti bolognese.

e) Fruit salad as a dessert.

3 🌐 **2.45 Listen to a conversation between Alan and Kathryn and check your answers to Exercise 2.**

What's Alan's 'seafood' diet?

Writing & Speaking

Work with a partner. Use the 'food-combining' rules to do the following tasks.

a) Write a menu for a 'healthy' day.

b) Write a menu for an 'unhealthy' day.

c) Decide which menu you like best.

Grammar

How much/many ...?

With countable nouns
How many apples are there?

●●● = There are a lot. /
●●●   A lot.

●● = There aren't many. /
   Not many.

○ = There aren't any. /
  None.

With uncountable nouns
How much cheese is there?

▬▬▬ = There's a lot. /
   A lot.

▬ = There isn't much. /
   Not much.

☐ = There isn't any. /
   None.

1   Look at the pictures and complete the questions and answers.

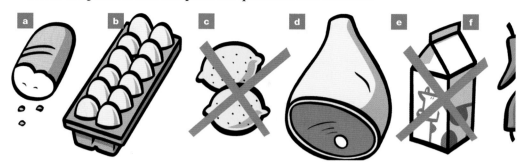

a)   '*How much* bread is there?'   'There *isn't much.*'
b)   'How _____ eggs are there?'   'There are _____ .'
c)   '_____ lemons are there?'   'There _____ .'
d)   '_____ meat is there?   'There _____ .'
e)   '_____ milk is there?'   'There _____ .'
f)   '_____ peppers are there?'   'There _____ .'

🔘 **2.46 Listen, check and repeat.**

2   **Think about what is in your fridge or kitchen at the moment. Work with a partner. Ask and answer the questions in Exercise 1.**

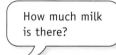

> How much milk is there?

> Not much.

> How many eggs are there?

> None.

Ask about other food and drink.

3 | **Pairwork**   **Student A:** page 119   **Student B:** page 124

4 | **Grammar** *Extra* **10** page 130. Read the explanation and do the exercises.

Speaking: anecdote

1   🔘 **2.47 Listen to Natalie talking about the last time she had a delicious meal. <u>Underline</u> the correct information.**

a)   'When did you have the meal?' 'We had the meal <u>**last weekend**</u> / **two weeks ago**.'
b)   'What was the occasion?' 'It was **a business dinner** / **my brother's 18th birthday**.'
c)   'Where did you have the meal?' 'We had the meal **at home** / **in an Italian restaurant**.'
d)   'How many people were there?' 'There were **fifteen of us** / **just two of us**.'
e)   'Who did you sit next to?' 'I sat next to **Alberto** / **my grandmother**.'
f)   'What did you eat?' 'I had **pizza** / **steak and chips**.'
g)   'How long did you stay at the table?' 'We stayed **for nearly three hours** / **all evening**.'
h)   'Did you have a good time?' 'It was **a really good evening** / **a really terrible evening**.'

2   **You're going to tell your partner about the last time you had a delicious meal.**
- Ask yourself the questions in Exercise 1.
- Think about *what* to say and *how* to say it.
- Tell your partner about the last time you had a delicious meal.

> The last time I had a delicious meal was ...

Useful phrases

1 🔊 2.48 **Listen to a conversation between a shop assistant (SA) and a customer (C).**

   a) What does the customer want to eat?

   b) How much does he pay?

2 **Complete the conversation with the words in the box.**

   | I'd   like   Would   you   you'd |

   SA: Next!

   C: (1) *I'd* like a chicken sandwich, please.

   SA: (2) _____ *you like* brown bread or white bread, butter or margarine, mustard or mayonnaise, salt and pepper?

   C: I'd (3) _____ ... a chicken sandwich.

   SA: Yes, I know (4) _____ like a chicken sandwich. But would you (5) _____ brown bread or white bread, butter ...?

   C: STOP, STOP! Can you speak more slowly, please?

   SA: Would (6) _____ like white or brown bread?

   C: Er ... brown bread, please.

   SA: (7) _____ you like butter or margarine?

   C: Butter.

   SA: Would you (8) _____ mustard or mayonnaise?

   C: Mayonnaise.

   SA: Would (9) _____ like salt and pepper?

   C: No, thank you.

   SA: (10) _____ you like anything to drink?

   C: Anything to drink? What is 'anything to drink'?

   SA: Coke, orange juice, water ...

   C: Ah, drink, drink – Coke, orange juice, water. Yes, yes, I understand. ... No.

   SA: That's five dollars. Next!

   Listen again and check your answers.

3 🔊 2.49 **Listen and repeat the useful phrases.**

   a) I'd like a chicken sandwich, please.

   b) Would you like brown bread or white bread?

   c) Can you speak more slowly, please?

   d) Would you like anything to drink?

   e) That's five dollars.

   Practise the conversation with a partner.

4 **Work with a partner. Write a new conversation about a customer who wants a chicken sandwich with white bread, margarine, mustard and salt and pepper and some water (= seven dollars).**

   Practise the conversation.

Vocabulary *Extra*

Food

1   Match the pictures with the food in each group.

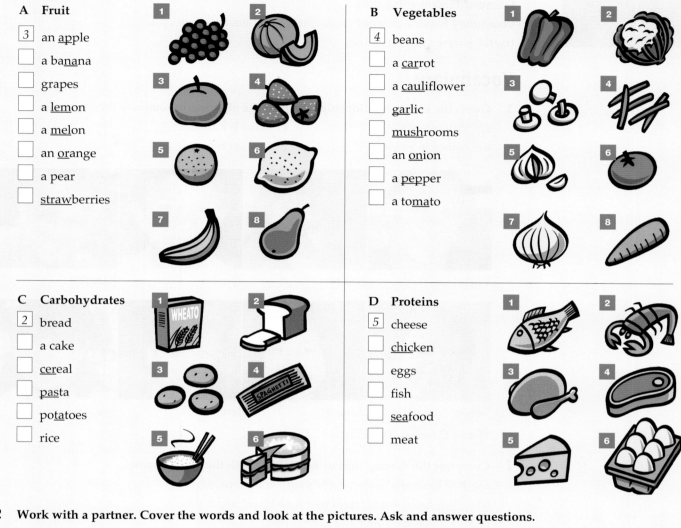

A   Fruit

[3] an <u>apple</u>
[ ] a ba<u>na</u>na
[ ] grapes
[ ] a <u>lemon</u>
[ ] a <u>melon</u>
[ ] an <u>orange</u>
[ ] a pear
[ ] <u>straw</u>berries

B   Vegetables

[4] beans
[ ] a <u>carrot</u>
[ ] a <u>cauliflower</u>
[ ] <u>garlic</u>
[ ] <u>mushrooms</u>
[ ] an <u>onion</u>
[ ] a <u>pepper</u>
[ ] a tomato

C   Carbohydrates

[2] bread
[ ] a cake
[ ] <u>cereal</u>
[ ] <u>pasta</u>
[ ] <u>potatoes</u>
[ ] rice

D   Proteins

[5] cheese
[ ] <u>chicken</u>
[ ] eggs
[ ] fish
[ ] <u>sea</u>food
[ ] meat

2   Work with a partner. Cover the words and look at the pictures. Ask and answer questions.

What's this?   A melon.   What are these?   Grapes.

Focus on prepositions of place (2)

1   Match the pictures with the sentences about the key.

[3] It's **on** the wall.
[ ] It's **in** the cupboard.
[ ] It's **on** the coffee table.
[ ] It's **under** the rug.
[ ] It's **above** the door.
[ ] It's **next to** the plant.

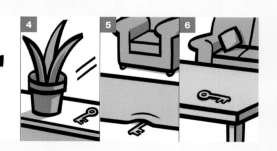

2   Ask your partner questions about the classroom.

Where's the clock?   It's on the wall above the door.

11 Looks

Grammar Present continuous
Vocabulary Physical description. Clothes. Plural nouns: *a pair of* ...
Useful phrases Buying clothes

Vocabulary

1 **Guess the family relationships. Look at the photos and complete the sentences.**

a) Will is Sue's *son*.

b) Nancy is Simon's _____ .

c) Gus is Zainab's _____ .

d) Albert is Jem's _____ .

Will   Nancy   Gus   Albert

Simon   Zainab   Jem   Sue

🔘 2.50 **Listen and check.**

2 **Complete the descriptions of each photo with the correct name.**

a) *Will* has a shaved head. He's very good-looking.

b) _____ has short, straight hair with blond highlights.

c) _____ has dark hair and green eyes.

d) _____ has short, grey hair.

e) _____ has dark brown eyes and short hair.

f) _____ has short, curly hair. She's very sweet.

g) _____ has medium-length, dark hair. She has a lovely smile.

h) _____ has very curly hair.

🔘 2.51 **Listen, check and repeat.**

3 **Complete the table with words and phrases from Exercise 2.**

Hair length	Hair colour	Hair style	Eyes	Opinion	Other
a shaved head	*dark*	*straight*	*green*	*very good-looking*	*a beard*

4 🔘 2.52 **Listen and repeat the words in the box. Then add them to the table in Exercise 3.**

> a beard beautiful blue fair handsome long a moustache a tattoo wavy

5 **Pairwork Student A:** page 119 **Student B:** page 124

Speaking

1 Work with a partner. Describe people in the class and guess their identity.

> She has long, straight hair and brown eyes. She has gold earrings.

> Maria.

> Yes, that's right. / No, that's wrong.

2 Write short descriptions of three people you know. Tell your partner about them.

Vocabulary

1 Look at the photograph of Stuart. Tick (✓) the items that you can see in the photo.

Clothes and accessories

Footwear
boots   shoes ✓   trainers

Underwear
socks   underpants

Formal clothes
coats   jackets ✓   shirts   suits   ties   trousers

Casual clothes
jeans   sweaters   tops   tracksuits   T-shirts

Accessories
belts   hats   rings   sunglasses

🔊 2.53 Listen and repeat all the words.

2 Complete the following table with clothes and accessories from Exercise 1.

A: Singular nouns (a …)	B: Plural nouns (a *pair of* …)
a coat, a jacket, …	*a pair of boots, a pair of shoes, …*

🔊 2.54 Listen, check and repeat.

Listening

1 🔊 2.55 Listen to an interview with Stuart. <u>Underline</u> the correct information.
a) He has **35** / **50** / <u>**350**</u> shirts.
b) He has **100** / **200** / **300** suits.
c) He has **50** / **115** / **150** pairs of trousers.
d) He has **25** / **100** / **125** pairs of shoes.

2 Work with a partner. Ask and answer questions.

> How many shirts do you have?

> Ten. How many … do you have?

Reading

1 Read and complete the magazine quiz about the average British man.

IMAGE

QUIZ OF THE MONTH

Win a fabulous prize!

1ST PRIZE
A weekend for two in the fashion capital of the world, Milan

2ND PRIZE
£1,000 to spend in the clothes shop of your choice

3RD PRIZE
A free year's subscription to *IMAGE*

Mr Average and his clothes

Choose the correct answers below.

How many items of clothing does Mr Average have?
1   a) 32 b) 22 c) 12 pairs of socks
2   a) 16 b) 12 c) 6 pairs of underpants
3   a) 25 b) 20 c) 15 casual tops
4   a) 13 b) 10 c) 8 formal shirts
5   a) 21 b) 17 c) 7 pairs of casual trousers
6   a) 16 b) 6 c) 3 pairs of formal trousers
7   a) 2 b) 4 c) 8 jackets

How much does Mr Average spend?
8   a) £550   b) £350   c) £250 a year on clothes
9   a) £140   b) £90   c) £40 a year on underwear
10   a) £150   b) £50   c) £15 a year on accessories
11   a) £300   b) £200   c) £100 a year on footwear
12   a) £1,500   b) £1,000   c) £500 a year on cigarettes and beer!!!

Put your answers on a post-card and send them to
'Quiz', IMAGE, PO Box 1480, London W1A 4WW

2 Compare your answers with a partner then look at the answers below.

1b 2a 3c 4a 5c 6b 7b 8b 9c 10b 11a 12c

3 Work with a partner. Refer to the *IMAGE* quiz and discuss the questions.
a)   How many items of clothing does Mr Average have in your country?
b)   Who has the most clothes in your family?
c)   How many items of clothing do you have?

Pronunciation

1 🔊 2.56 Listen and repeat the chants.

A	B
jeans and jackets	shoes and socks
belts and boots	shirts and suits
casual clothes	formal clothes
casual clothes	formal clothes

2 Complete the table with the plural nouns in the chant.

Plural nouns ending in /s/	Plural nouns ending in /z/
jackets	*jeans*

Practise the chants.

Listening

1 🔘 **2.57 Listen to a radio commentator, Ross White, describing people as they arrive for the Oscars ceremony in Hollywood. Put the photos (a–c) in the right order (1–3).**

▼ Keira Knightley

▼ Jake Gyllenhaal

▼ Charlize Theron

2 Match the verb phrases in column *A* with the noun phrases in column *B*.

A	B
a) I'm waiting for	around.
b) She's wearing	at everybody.
c) She's turning	a beautiful red dress.
d) He's wearing	the big stars.
e) He's smiling	a black bow tie.

Listen again and check. Who is doing each action?

Grammar

Present continuous

I'm
You're
He's
She's   working.
It's
We're
They're

Are you **working**?
Yes, I **am**.
No, I'm **not**.

Is she **working**?
Yes, she **is**.
No, she **isn't**.

1 Complete the questions and answers with a pronoun and the correct form of *be*.

a) '*Are* you wearing jeans?'   'Yes, *I am.*'   'No, *I'm not.*'
b) '_____ you sitting next to a window?'   'Yes, _____ .'   'No, _____ .'
c) '_____ your teacher standing up?'   'Yes, _____ .'   'No, _____ .'
d) '_____ the traffic making a noise?'   'Yes, _____ .'   'No, _____ .'
e) '_____ you all wearing watches?'   'Yes, _____ .'   'No, _____ .'
f) '_____ the birds singing outside?'   'Yes, _____ .'   'No, _____ .'

🔘 **2.58 Listen, check and repeat.**

2 Work with a partner. Ask and answer the questions in Exercise 1.

3 Think of three people in your family. Guess what they are doing at the moment. Tell your partner.

> I think my father is working. My sister is doing her homework, and my brother is playing his guitar.

4 Grammar *Extra* **11** page 130. Read the explanation and do the exercises.

Useful phrases

1 **Look at the illustration. Circle the kind of clothes you can see.**

  a) sports clothes b) suits c) evening dresses d) baby clothes

2 🔵 **2.59 Read and listen to the conversation between a customer (*Erica*) and a shop assistant (*SA*). What colour dress does Erica choose?**

SA: Can I help you, madam?
Erica: No, I'm just looking, thank you.
SA: Are you looking for anything special?
Erica: Yes, I'm looking for a dress. I'm going to a party.
SA: Oh, lovely. Evening dresses are over here, madam.
Erica: Thank you.
SA: What colour are you looking for?
Erica: I don't know.
SA: How about this pink one?
Erica: Oh no, I don't like pink.
SA: OK. How about this yellow one, madam?
Erica: Oh no, not yellow, thank you.
SA: Right. We have a lovely red dress here.
Erica: Red? Er ... no. Not red.
SA: Blue?
Erica: No.
SA: Green?
Erica: Er ... no. Do you have this dress in a medium?
SA: Ah, the black dress. Yes, madam. Here you are.
Erica: Thank you. Can I try it on?
SA: Certainly, madam. The changing rooms are over there.

3 **Cover up the conversation above. Who says the useful phrases? Write *E* for Erica and *SA* for the shop assistant.**

  a) Can I help you? *SA*
  b) No, I'm just looking, thank you.
  c) I'm looking for a dress.
  d) What colour are you looking for?
  e) How about this yellow one, madam?
  f) Do you have this dress in a medium?
  g) Can I try it on?
  h) The changing rooms are over there.

🔵 **2.60 Listen, check and repeat.**

4 **Work with a partner. Choose a situation and write a conversation.**

  a) A man is choosing a shirt.
  b) A woman is choosing a pair of shoes.
  c) A teenager is choosing a T-shirt.

Practise the conversation.

Vocabulary *Extra*

Clothes

1 Match the pictures with the words.

- [6] a belt
- [ ] boots
- [ ] a coat
- [ ] a hat
- [ ] a jacket
- [ ] a shirt
- [ ] a skirt
- [ ] shoes
- [ ] socks
- [ ] a suit
- [ ] a top
- [ ] a tracksuit
- [ ] trainers
- [ ] trousers
- [ ] a T-shirt

2 Work with a partner. Cover the words and look at the pictures. Ask and answer questions.

> What's this?

> It's a coat.

> What are these?

> They're boots.

Focus on *get*

1 Complete the table with the phrases in the box.

> get an email   get home   get a job   get married   ~~get a new car~~   get up at 7.00 a.m.

Some uses of *get*	Examples
a) *get* + noun = buy, obtain or receive	get a text message (1) *get a new car* (2) _____ (3) _____
b) *get* = arrive	get to work (4) _____
c) expressions with *get*	get dressed get divorced (5) _____
d) phrasal verbs with *get*	get on a bus (6) _____

2 Write your own example sentence for each use of *get*.

12 Money

Grammar Comparative and superlative adjectives
Vocabulary Money. Big numbers
Useful phrases Describing objects

Reading

1 🌐 **2.61 Read the article about Karyn. What was Karyn's problem?**

savekaryn.com

Karyn was living in New York. She had a good job and she earned a good salary. But she didn't save her money. She spent it on clothes, shoes and cosmetics. Every time she went
5   shopping she used a credit card, and soon she had a debt of $20,000. Then she lost her job.

  She found another job, but the salary was lower. She couldn't pay her bills.

  She moved to a smaller flat, bought cheaper
10 clothes and was more careful with her money, but she still had a huge credit card debt. Then she had a brilliant idea. She started a website called savekaryn.com and put this letter on it.

Hello everyone,

15 *Thank you all for visiting my website! My name is Karyn and I'm asking for your help. I need $20,000 to pay my credit card bill. I need $1 from 20,000 people, or $2 from 10,000 people, or $5 from 4,000 people. SO I'M ASKING … Give me $1. Give me $5.*
20 *Give me $20 if you want!*

And they did. In fact, they sent her $13,323.08 in total, and in five months she paid her credit card bill.

  Now Karyn doesn't have any debts and she's an internet celebrity. First she wrote a book called *Save Karyn*, and
25 now Hollywood want to make a film about her.

2 **Are these sentences about Karyn true or false?**

a) She spent all her money on her family. *False*

b) She had a very big credit card debt.

c) Her new job was better than her old job.

d) She started a website.

e) People sent her money to pay her credit card bill.

f) She has more debts now than before.

3 **Put the following items in the correct order to make a summary of the article.**

☐ a) a book about her experience.

2 b) loved shopping. She used her credit

☐ c) debt. Then she lost her job. She couldn't pay

☐ d) people for money. After five months she

☐ e) card a lot and soon she had a huge

1 f) Karyn had a good job but she

☐ g) paid her credit card bill. Then she wrote

☐ h) her bills, so she started a website and asked

🌐 **2.62 Listen and check.**

Vocabulary

1 Complete each sentence with a word from the article on page 78.

a) I never *save* money. I always spend all my money. (line 3)

b) I _____ a lot of money last weekend. (line 3)

c) My _____ was lower five years ago. (line 7)

d) I always pay my _____ on time. (line 8)

e) I never use my _____ card to buy things on the internet. (line 11)

🔊 2.63 **Listen, check and repeat.**

2 Tick (✓) the sentences in Exercise 1 that are true for you. Compare with a partner.

Grammar

Comparative adjectives

Short adjectives: + *er*
cheap ➔ cheap**er**
nice ➔ nic**er**
big ➔ big**ger**
lucky ↓ luck**ier**

Long adjectives:
more **+ adjective**
careful ➔ **more** careful
beautiful ➔ **more** beautiful

Irregular forms
good ➔ better
bad ➔ worse
far ➔ further

1 <u>Underline</u> the comparative adjectives in this sentence from the article about Karyn.

She moved to a <u>smaller</u> flat, bought cheaper clothes and was more careful with her money.

2 Complete the table with comparative forms of the adjectives in the box.

~~beautiful~~ big clean fast good happy important interesting old rich

Short adjectives (+ *er*)	Long adjectives (*more* + adjective)	Irregular forms
	more beautiful	

🔊 2.64 **Listen, check and repeat.**

3 Write three sentences about things you'd like to have. Combine comparative adjectives from Exercise 2 with nouns in the box, or your own ideas.

a boyfriend / girlfriend   a car   a house   a job

> 1 I'd like a richer boyfriend
> 2 I'd like a faster car.
> 3 I'd like a more interesting job.

Compare your sentences with a partner.

4 Work with a partner. Complete the sentences with the correct form of the adjective.

a) I'm *taller* than Alex. (tall)

b) I'm _____ than Carole. (old)

c) My handwriting is _____ than Gina's. (bad)

d) My mobile phone is _____ than Eddie's. (small)

e) My house is _____ the school than Ian's. (far from)

f) My pen was _____ than Kerry's. (expensive)

🔊 2.65 **Listen, check and repeat.**

5 Replace the names in Exercise 4 with the names of people in the class or people you know. Make true sentences.

Make more true sentences with the adjectives in the box.

big   cheap   good   near to   short   young

My bag is bigger than Paul's.

Me

Alex

Pronunciation

1 🔊 2.66 Listen and repeat the chants. How do you pronounce the vowel sound in red?

A
I'm taller than my sister.
I'm taller than my brother.
I'm taller than my mother.
I'm very, very tall!

B
I'm younger than my teacher.
I'm younger than my doctor.
I'm younger than my neighbour.
I'm very, very young!

2 Which lines in the chants are true for you?

Vocabulary & Listening

1 Write the prices in full. Notice when you use *and*.

a) $1,250,620 *One million, two hundred <u>and</u> fifty thousand, six hundred <u>and</u> twenty dollars*
b) $85,590
c) $11,302,650
d) $65,208

🔊 2.67 Listen, check and repeat.

2 Work with a partner. Match the things (*1–4*) with the prices (*a–d*) in Exercise 1.

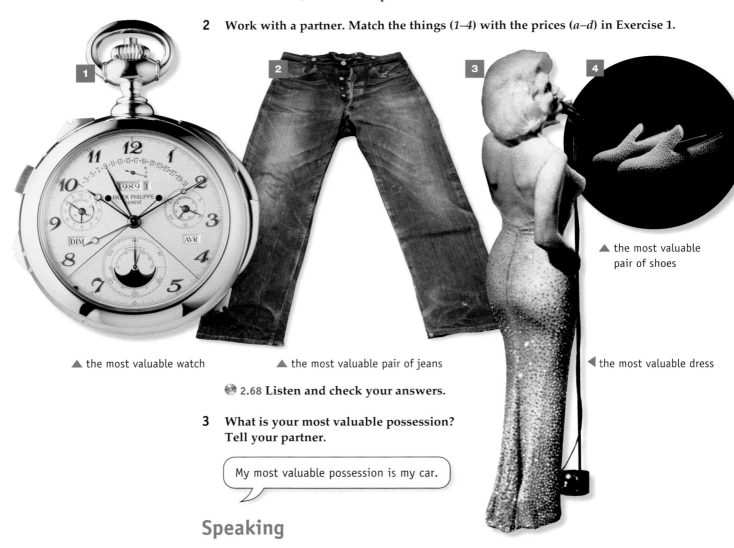

1
▲ the most valuable watch

2
▲ the most valuable pair of jeans

3

4
▲ the most valuable pair of shoes

◀ the most valuable dress

🔊 2.68 Listen and check your answers.

3 What is your most valuable possession? Tell your partner.

> My most valuable possession is my car.

Speaking

1 Write how much you usually pay for the following things.

a) a pair of shoes
b) a pair of jeans
c) a jacket or a coat
d) a present for a friend
e) a meal in a restaurant
f) a haircut

2 Compare your answers with a partner.

Grammar

Superlative adjectives

Short adjectives:
the + est

young ➔ the young**est**
nice ➔ the nic**est**
bi**g** ➔ the big**gest**
ug**ly** ➔ the ugl**iest**

Long adjectives:
the most + adjective

famous ➔
the most famous
expensive ➔
the most expensive

Irregular forms

good ➔ the best
bad ➔ the worst
far ➔ the furthest

1 Complete the questions about your family with superlative adjectives.

a) Who's *the youngest*? (young)
b) Who's _____ ? (old)
c) Who's _____ ? (interesting)
d) Who's _____ ? (lucky)
e) Who's _____ ? (bad driver)
f) Who's _____ ? (good cook)

🌐 **2.69 Listen, check and repeat.**

2 Work with a partner. Ask and answer the questions in Exercise 1 about your family.

> Who's the youngest person in your family?

> My niece, Magda. She's five months old.

3 Pairwork **Student A:** page 119 **Student B:** page 124

4 Grammar *Extra* 12 page 130. Read the explanation and do the exercises.

Reading

1 Look at the objects. In your opinion, which are the most common things to lose?

| a keys | b a TV re**mote** con**trol** | c a **hand**bag | d a pet snake |

| e **mo**ney | f a **mobile phone** | g **glasses** | h a **pass**port |

2 🌐 **2.70 Read the article and check your ideas.**

Lost property

The average person in Britain spends a year of their life looking for lost objects. Monday is the most common day to lose things.

Research at the University of Central Lancashire shows what men and women do when they lose things. One in five women cry, and more than a quarter of men swear. Some women become violent.

The objects that people are most likely to lose are money, keys and the TV remote control. People hardly ever lose their passport.

Half the people interviewed said they would like to lose boring friends!

3 Work in small groups. Discuss the questions.

a) Which things from Exercise 1 do you have with you now / at home / at work or school?
b) Which things do you often lose / sometimes lose / never lose?
c) When was the last time you lost something? What happened? Where did you find it?

Useful phrases

1 🔊 **2.71 Read and listen to Judy's conversation with a Lost Property Officer (*LPO*). Answer the questions.**

a) Which bag (*1–3*) did Judy lose?
b) What was in Judy's bag?

LPO: Lost Property Office. Can I help you?
Judy: Oh, um, hello ... I'm ringing because I lost my bag yesterday.
LPO: I see. Well, there are thirty-eight bags here. What colour is it and what's it made of?
Judy: Oh yes, um ... It's black and it's made of leather.
LPO: Hm ... black ... leather ... There are twenty-four black leather bags here. So what kind of bag is it?
Judy: It's a handbag. A small handbag.
LPO: Is there anything in it?
Judy: Yes, there's a mobile phone, and some glasses. Oh, and Hissy.
LPO: Hissy?
Judy: Yes, Hissy the snake.
LPO: There's a snake ... in your bag?
Judy: Yes, but don't worry, it's made of plastic. It belongs to my five-year-old son.
LPO: Right, well, I think we have your bag here. The office is open from nine in the morning until ...

2 Match the questions with possible answers. <u>Underline</u> the answers Judy gives in the conversation.

a) What colour is it?   1 It's a shopping bag / a shoulder bag / a handbag.
b) What's it made of?   2 It's black / red / white.
c) What kind of bag is it?   3 There's a passport / a pen / a plastic snake.
d) Is there anything in it?   4 It's made of leather / plastic / nylon.

🔊 **2.72 Listen, check and repeat the useful phrases.**

3 Work with a partner. Imagine you lost your own bag. Write a conversation between you and a Lost Property Officer.

Practise the conversation.

Vocabulary *Extra*

Common adjectives

1 Match the pictures with the adjectives.

- 10 big
- ☐ <u>boring</u>
- ☐ cheap
- ☐ <u>difficult</u>
- ☐ <u>dirty</u>
- ☐ <u>early</u>
- ☐ fast
- ☐ good
- ☐ <u>happy</u>
- ☐ long
- ☐ loud
- ☐ <u>lucky</u>
- ☐ rich
- ☐ <u>ugly</u>
- ☐ young

2 Match the adjectives in the box with their opposites in Exercise 1.

bad – good

> ~~bad~~   <u>beautiful</u>   clean   <u>easy</u>   exp<u>en</u>sive   <u>interesting</u>   late   old   poor
> <u>quiet</u>   sad   short   slow   small   un<u>lucky</u>

3 Work with a partner. Ask and answer questions.

> What's the opposite of *dirty?*

> *Clean.* What's the opposite of *poor?*

Focus on *like*

1 Complete the table with the phrases in the box.

> ~~Do you like sushi?~~   I don't like washing up.   She doesn't like him.
> They'd like a holiday.   They like cooking.

Some uses of *like*	Examples
a) *like* + noun = ☺	I really like Picasso. I don't like it. (1) *Do you like sushi?* (2) _____
b) *like* + *ing* = enjoy an activity	We like sailing. He likes going out. (3) _____ (4) _____
c) *would like* + noun = want something	I'd like a chicken sandwich. Would you like a drink? (5) _____

2 Write your own example sentence for each use of *like*.

Review C

Grammar

▶ Grammar *Extra* pages 130 and 131

1 Write four countable nouns and four uncountable nouns under each heading.

▲ apples   ▲ meat   ▲ strawberries

▲ milk   ▲ bananas   ▲ water   ▲ eggs   ▲ bread

Countable	Uncountable
apples	*meat*

2 Look at the pictures in Exercise 1 and complete the conversation. Use the words in the box.

~~Are~~ are is is isn't lot many much

Mary: (1) *Are* there any eggs?

Tom: Yes, there (2) _____ .

Mary: How (3) _____ ?

Tom: A (4) _____ .

Mary: And (5) _____ there any milk?

Tom: Yes, there (6) _____ .

Mary: How (7) _____ ?

Tom: There (8) _____ much.

Work with a partner. Have similar conversations about other items in the pictures.

3 Complete the sentences with the verbs (in brackets) in the present continuous form.

a) I (wear) *'m wearing* a T-shirt.

b) My parents (work) _____ today.

c) Our teacher (talk) _____ to us.

d) I (sit) _____ near the door.

e) I (read) _____ a newspaper.

f) I (hold) _____ a pencil.

Rewrite the sentences in the negative.

a) I'm not wearing a T-shirt.

Tick (✓) the sentences (affirmative and negative) which are true for you. Compare with a partner.

4 Complete the sentences with the comparative form of the adjectives.

a) Angelina Jolie is (beautiful) *more beautiful* than Julia Roberts.

b) Clothes are (cheap) _____ in Rome than in Paris.

c) Brad Pitt is a (good) _____ actor than Jake Gyllenhaal.

d) Madrid is a (nice) _____ city than London.

e) Football is (interesting) _____ than golf.

f) Keira Knightley is a (big) _____ star than Charlize Theron.

Work with a partner. Discuss each statement. Do you agree or disagree?

5 Write the superlative form of each adjective.

a) Who's the (tall) *tallest* woman in the class?

b) Who's the (young) _____ man in the class?

c) Who has the (good) _____ handwriting in the class?

d) Who's wearing the (interesting) _____ clothes in the class?

e) Whose home is the (far) _____ from the school?

f) Who has the (lovely) _____ smile in the class?

Work with a partner. Discuss possible answers to the questions.

I think Irina is the tallest woman.

6 Spot the mistake! Cross out the incorrect sentence, *a* or *b*.

1 a) ~~I working with my father today.~~
   b) I'm working with my father today.

2 a) You are studying Spanish?
   b) Are you studying Spanish?

3 a) He is better than me at sport.
   b) He is better as me at sport.

4 a) I'm the happiest person in the world!
   b) I'm the most happiest person in the world!

5 a) There aren't some curtains.
   b) There aren't any curtains.

6 a) Is there any cheese?
   b) Are there any cheese?

Vocabulary

1 Look at the picture of a living room. <u>Underline</u> the things in the box that you can see.

> armchair bath bed bookcase coffee table
> cooker cupboard curtains cushions
> fridge lamp mirror picture plant
> rug shower sofa washbasin

2 <u>Underline</u> the 'odd thing out' in each room.

a) in the bedroom: bookcase, lamp, bed, bath
b) in the kitchen: fridge, cupboard, shower, picture
c) in the bathroom: washbasin, curtains, mirror, cooker

Compare your answers with a partner.

3 <u>Underline</u> the correct prepositions.

We have two homes. Our first home is (1) **in** / **on** the city. We live (2) **in** / **on** an apartment, (3) **in** / **on** the top floor. Our city is (4) **in** / **near** the coast. Our second home is (5) **near** / **on** a small village (6) **in** / **on** the mountains. There's a small river (7) **in** / **near** our house. I love life (8) **in** / **on** the country!

Work with a partner. Describe to your partner where your home is.

4 Read the clues and find the names of the types of food.

> apple banana bread carrot cheese egg
> fish orange ~~pasta~~ potato rice

a) Italy's favourite carbohydrate. *pasta*
b) A red or green fruit.
c) A long, yellow fruit.
d) You make sandwiches with this carbohydrate.
e) You make chips with this.
f) Asia's favourite carbohydrate.
g) An orange vegetable.
h) This form of protein makes an omelette.
i) A form of protein from the sea.
j) A form of protein from milk.
k) A round, orange fruit.

5 Complete the descriptions with the words in the box.

> ~~beautiful~~ belt green jeans
> rings straight trainers T-shirt

She's a (1) *beautiful* woman with long, (2) _____ hair and (3) _____ eyes. She's wearing a white (4) _____ and a pair of (5) _____ with a brown (6) _____ . She's wearing a pair of white (7) _____ and she has a lot of (8) _____ on her fingers.

> blue grey handsome shirt
> shoes smile suit tie

He has short, (9) _____ hair and (10) _____ eyes. He isn't (11) _____ , but he has a lovely (12) _____ . He's wearing a dark (13) _____ , a white (14) _____ , a red (15) _____ and a beautiful pair of Italian (16) _____ .

6 Match the amounts of money in figures (*a–e*) with the amounts in words (*1–5*). Practise saying the amounts.

a) $1,100
b) $11,100
c) $1,100,000
d) $11,100,000
e) $111,100,000

1 one million, one hundred thousand dollars
2 eleven million, one hundred thousand dollars
3 one thousand, one hundred dollars
4 one hundred and eleven million, one hundred thousand dollars
5 eleven thousand, one hundred dollars

Pronunciation

1 Look at some words from Units 9–12. Say the words and add them to the table.

> ~~armchair~~ ~~banana~~ ~~beautiful~~ curly
> expensive garlic important interesting
> lemon ~~moustache~~ potato salary
> tattoo vegetable

A: ☐☐	B: ☐☐☐	C: ☐☐	D: ☐☐☐
<u>arm</u>chair	<u>beau</u>tiful	mous<u>tache</u>	ba<u>na</u>na

2 <u>Underline</u> the stressed syllable in each word.

🎧 3.01 **Listen, check and repeat.**

Reading & Listening

1 🌐 3.02 **Read the descriptions of three restaurants. Are the sentences true or false?**

a) The Fat Duck is in a new building. *False*

b) There isn't any fish on the menu at the Fat Duck.

c) Ferran Adrià is especially famous for his traditional dishes.

d) El Bulli is a small restaurant.

e) The beef at Aragawa comes from cows that drink beer.

f) Aragawa is famous for its chips.

2 **Work with a partner. Choose one of the restaurants in Exercise 1 for these people. Say why you chose it.**

a) Someone who doesn't eat meat.

b) Someone who is very rich.

c) Someone who lives near London.

Which restaurant would *you* like to eat in?

3 **What is your favourite restaurant? Describe it to your partner.**

4 🌐 3.03 **Listen to the phone conversation and complete the information about Lara's reservation.**

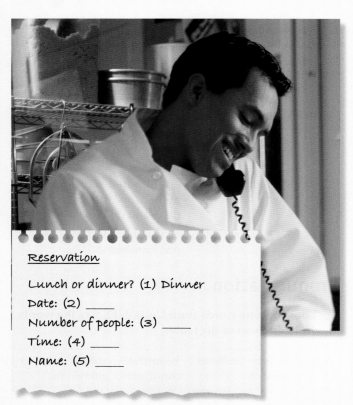

Reservation

Lunch or dinner? (1) Dinner

Date: (2) _____

Number of people: (3) _____

Time: (4) _____

Name: (5) _____

5 <u>Underline</u> **the correct answers.**

a) There aren't any tables for **lunch** / <u>**dinner**</u> on Friday.

b) It's Lara's birthday on **Friday** / **Saturday**.

c) There **are some** / **aren't any** window tables for dinner on Saturday.

d) You **can** / **can't** see the river from the restaurant.

e) Dress at the restaurant is **casual** / **formal**.

f) The restaurant **takes** / **doesn't take** credit cards.

The most famous
RESTAURANTS
in the world

These three restaurants are some of the best and most famous restaurants in the world.

The Fat Duck, Bray, England

This 450-year-old pub is in a village near London. The owner of The Fat Duck, Heston Blumental, taught himself to cook. He cooks food that is delicious and fun. There's steak, chicken and fish on the menu, but also more unusual things like bacon and egg ice cream!

Dress: casual   Cost: about £80 per person

El Bulli, Ala Montjoi, Spain

Some people think the chef at this restaurant, Ferran Adrià, is the best cook in the world. El Bulli is on the coast, about two hours from Barcelona, and it has wonderful views of the sea. It's very difficult to get a reservation because it's only open for six months of the year, and there are only fifty seats. But the food is amazing! The menu has a lot of traditional vegetable and seafood dishes, but it's especially famous for its strange dishes like bread with oil and chocolate!

Dress: casual   Cost: about £150 per person

Aragawa, Tokyo, Japan

This is the most expensive restaurant in the world! It was the first steakhouse in Japan and it's famous for its beef steak. The beef comes from cows which live near Tokyo. The beef tastes so good because the cows drink beer! At Aragawa you don't eat the steak with chips. It comes with only pepper and mustard.

Dress: formal   Cost: about £300 per person

Writing & Speaking

1 Read the email. How does Patricia start and end the email?

> Dear Mum and Dad
>
> ① I'm sitting here, feeling very relaxed and looking at the beautiful, blue sea.
>
> ② We're staying at the Palm Beach Hotel. It's amazing! There are two white sofas in our room and a big plasma TV in our bathroom! The shower is outside, under the trees.
>
> ③ It's really quiet here. There aren't any cars on the island, and there aren't many people at the hotel.
>
> ④ Yesterday we went to a market in a village and ate at a fantastic restaurant on the beach. We're having a great time.
>
> See you soon.
> Love, Patricia

2 Read the email again. Which paragraph describes these things? Write the paragraph number.

a) Where Patricia is staying. 2
b) What she's doing now.
c) What she did yesterday.
d) What the place is like.

3 Make a list of all the adjectives Patricia uses in the email.

4 Work with a partner. Imagine you are on a lovely holiday now. Ask and answer questions about your holiday.

a) What / doing now?
b) Where / staying?
c) What / the place like?
d) What / do yesterday?

Is your holiday similar to your partner's?

5 Write an email about the holiday you imagined in Exercise 4. Write four paragraphs. Use adjectives to describe your holiday.

🎵 3.04 **Song:** *Sailing*

13 Talent

Grammar *can* (for ability). Adverbs of manner. Frequency expressions
Vocabulary Character adjectives
Useful phrases Making excuses

Listening

1 Work with a partner. Match the photos (*1–4*) with the names.
What do you know about these famous people?

☐ Bono ☐ Shakira ☐ Bruce Willis ☐ Madonna

2 You are going to listen to a radio show called *Hidden talents*. Guess which famous person from Exercise 1 can do the following things.

a) _____ can play the harmonica.

b) _____ can play chess.

c) _____ can speak five languages.

d) _____ can ride a horse.

🌐 3.05 **Listen and check your ideas.**

Grammar

can/can't

Can you play poker?
Yes, I **can**.
No, I **can't**.
(can**'t** = can**not**)

1 Complete the questions and answers.

a) '*Can* you play the harmonica?'   'Yes, *I can.*'   'No, *I can't.*'

b) '*Can* your father play chess?'   'Yes, *he* _____.'   'No, *he* _____.'

c) '_____ you speak five languages?'   '_____.'   '_____.'

d) '_____ your mother ride a horse?'   '_____.'   '_____.'

e) '_____ you dance flamenco?'   '_____.'   '_____.'

f) '_____ your parents ski?'   '_____.'   '_____.'

🌐 3.06 **Listen, check and repeat.**

2 Work with a partner. Ask and answer the questions in Exercise 1.

3 Grammar *Extra* 13 page 132. Read the explanation and do the exercises.

Pronunciation

1 🌐 3.07 **Listen and repeat the chants. Notice the <u>stress</u>.**

A	B	C
I can <u>ski</u>, I can <u>swim</u>,	<u>Can</u> she <u>ski</u>? <u>Can</u> she <u>swim</u>?	He <u>can't</u> <u>ski</u>. He <u>can't</u> <u>swim</u>.
I can <u>dance</u>, I can <u>sing</u>.	<u>Can</u> she <u>dance</u>? <u>Can</u> she <u>sing</u>?	He <u>can't</u> <u>dance</u>. He <u>can't</u> <u>sing</u>.
<u>What</u> can <u>you</u> do?	<u>Yes</u>, she <u>can</u>.	<u>No</u>, he <u>can't</u>.
<u>What</u> can <u>you</u> do?	<u>Yes</u>, she <u>can</u>.	<u>No</u>, he <u>can't</u>.

2 **In which chant(s) is *can/can't* stressed? In which chant(s) is *can/can't* not stressed?**

Practise the chants in Exercise 1.

Grammar

Adverbs of manner

Adjective + *ly*
slow → slow**ly**
careful → careful**ly**
happy → happ**ily**

Irregular forms
good → well
fast → fast

1 **Complete each sentence with a verb phrase from the box or your own ideas.**

> cook   dance   draw   drive
> play football   play the
> piano   sing   ski   swim

a) I can _____ very well.

b) I can _____ quite well.

c) I can't _____ very well.

2 **Match the adjectives with the corresponding adverbs.**

Adjective	Adverb
bad	loudly
careful	slowly
fast	badly
good	happily
happy	fast
loud	quietly
quiet	well
slow	carefully

Answer the questions.

a) How do you form most adverbs?

b) Which adverbs are irregular?

'I can't cook very well!'

3 **Put the words in the correct order.**

subject + verb + object + adverb
I   eat   my food   very slowly.

a) I / very slowly / eat / my food

b) I / drive / quite fast / my car

c) I / play / very badly / the guitar

d) I / my money / spend / very carefully

e) I / very loudly / the drums / play

f) I / don't eat / very quietly / my soup

g) I / very happily / do / my homework

h) I / don't speak / very well / English

🌐 3.08 **Listen, check and repeat.**

How many sentences are true for you? Compare with a partner.

Reading

1 How many different types of dance do you know? Make a list (*salsa, disco ...*).

2 🔵 3.09 Read the article about Joaquín Cortés. Complete the headings with the words in the box.

> ~~Early life~~   Family   Hidden talents   Meals   Practice   Sleep   Travel

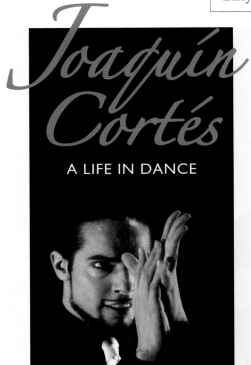

Joaquín Cortés

A LIFE IN DANCE

a) Early life
Joaquín Cortés was born in 1969 in Córdoba, southern Spain. He later moved to Madrid and started dancing when he was twelve. When he was fifteen he joined Spain's National Ballet company.

b) _____
In 1992 he started his own dance company. Now he travels all the time. He dances flamenco all over the world – every week he performs in a different city.

c) _____
He sleeps for five or six hours a night and wakes up full of energy.

d) _____
He practises for more than five hours a day. He buys a new pair of flamenco shoes every month.

e) _____
He loves good, healthy food. He eats three times a day.

f) _____
His family is the most important thing to him – he calls them every day.

g) _____
Joaquín Cortés is famous for his dancing, but he has many other talents. He can act, compose music and play the drums.

3 Match the beginnings and the endings of these sentences according to the article.

a) He travels ——————— five hours a day.
b) He sleeps for ——————— all the time.
c) He practises for more than   three times a day.
d) He buys new shoes   every day.
e) He eats   five or six hours a night.
f) He calls his family   every month.

🔵 3.10 Listen and check.

Grammar

Frequency expressions

Frequent

⬆

all the time
once a day
every week
twice a month
every year
every four years
never

⬇

Not frequent

1 Number the expressions in the box in order of frequency from *Frequent* (1) to *Not frequent* (6).

> every two weeks ☐   every day ☐   once a month ☐   three times a day ☐1
> twice a week ☐   four times a year ☐6

🔵 3.11 Listen, check and repeat.

2 Complete the questions with the missing word in the correct place.

a) How often you travel? (do)   *How often do you travel?*
b) How do you buy new shoes? (often)
c) How often do call your family? (you)

🔵 3.12 Listen, check and repeat. Ask your partner the questions.

3   **Pairwork** **Student A:** page 120   **Student B:** page 125

Vocabulary

1 Match the adjectives with the meanings.

a) <u>con</u>fident   1   You give a lot of time and/or money to people.
b) <u>gen</u>erous   2   You are nervous about meeting people.
c) <u>sel</u>fish   3   You are very sure of yourself.
d) <u>sen</u>sible   4   You think about things and don't laugh much.
e) <u>se</u>rious   5   You don't think about other people.
f)   shy   6   You never do stupid things.

🎧 3.13 **Listen and check.**

Which adjective always has a negative meaning?

2 Which three adjectives best describe you? Use adjectives from Exercise 1 or your own ideas.

Compare with a partner.

Reading

1 Read and complete the questionnaire.

What does your score mean? Compare with a partner.

HOW DO PEOPLE
really see you?

1 What's your favourite time of day?
  a) Morning.
  b) Afternoon and early evening.
  c) Night.

2 You usually walk ...
  a) very fast.
  b) quite fast.
  c) quite slowly.
  d) very slowly.

3 You usually speak ...
  a) fast and loudly.
  b) fast and quietly.
  c) slowly and loudly.
  d) slowly and quietly.

4 Which of these colours do you like the most?
  a) Red or orange.
  b) Black.
  c) Yellow or light blue.
  d) Green.
  e) Dark blue or purple.
  f) White.
  g) Brown or grey.

5 What's your favourite sleeping position?
  a) On your back.
  b) On your stomach.
  c) On your side.

How to score

1 a) 2   b) 4   c) 6
2 a) 6   b) 4   c) 3   d) 2
3 a) 4   b) 3   c) 5   d) 2
4 a) 6   b) 7   c) 5   d) 4
   e) 3   f) 2   g) 1
5 a) 7   b) 6   c) 4

What your score means

26 or more: People think you're confident, but also selfish. They admire you but they don't enjoy your company.

21–25: People think you're interesting and funny. They love being in your company.

16–20: People think you're friendly and generous.

11–15: People think you're unfriendly, but in fact you're just shy.

10 or less: People think you're quiet, serious and very sensible. They think you prefer to spend time alone.

2 Write descriptions of three people you know well. Begin with *People think ...*

People think my aunt Eva is friendly and generous ...

Useful phrases

1 **Match the top six excuses for not doing exercise (*a–f*) with the pictures (*1–6*).**

    a) 'I have a bad back.'
    b) 'I don't have time.'
    c) 'I'm really tired.'
    d) 'I have a cold.'
    e) 'I have a headache.'
    f) 'I don't have any money.'

     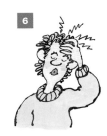

🔊 **3.14 Listen check and repeat.**

2 🔊 **3.15 Read and listen to the conversation. Tick (✓) the excuses in Exercise 1 that Lisa uses.**

Dan: Do you want to come to the gym later?
Lisa: Oh no, I can't. I'm really tired.
Dan: What about tomorrow?
Lisa: No, I can't. I have a bad back.
Dan: You should go swimming – swimming is really good for your back.
Lisa: I can't go swimming, I have a cold.
Dan: Oh dear. Well, you should have a massage.
Lisa: I can't, I don't have any money.
Dan: Do you want to go for a walk on Sunday?
Lisa: No, I can't.
Dan: Don't tell me – you have a bad foot.
Lisa: No, I can't go for a walk because I'm going shopping.
Dan: But you don't have any money.
Lisa: What?
Dan: Nothing.

3 🔊 **3.16 Listen and repeat the useful phrases.**

    a) Do you want to come to the gym?
    b) No, I can't.
    c) I'm really tired.
    d) What about tomorrow?
    e) I have a bad back.
    f) You should go swimming.

4 **Work with a partner. Write a similar conversation to the one in Exercise 2. Use your favourite excuses for not doing exercise.**

Practise your conversation.

Vocabulary *Extra*

Common adverbs

1 Match the pictures with the sentences.

- 3 She's driving carefully.
- ☐ He's winning easily.
- ☐ She's typing fast.
- ☐ They're playing happily.
- ☐ He's working hard.
- ☐ He's laughing loudly.
- ☐ She's reading quietly.
- ☐ He's speaking slowly.
- ☐ He's singing well.

2 Work with a partner. Cover the sentences and look at the pictures. Ask and answer questions.

> What's he doing?

> He's working hard. What's she doing?

Focus on *be*

1 Complete the table with the phrases in the box.

> Be careful!   He's twenty-one.   I'm cold.   ~~She's an architect.~~   There are some new students.
> They're bored.   We're waiting for a bus.

Some uses of *be*	Examples
a) *be* + *a/an* + job	I'm a teacher. He's a doctor. (1) *She's an architect.*
b) *be* + age* / height	I'm forty-six. She's 1 metre 68. (2) _____
c) *be* + feelings / physical states**	She's happy. We're thirsty. (3) _____ (4) _____
d) *be* + adjective = imperative	Be quiet! Don't be stupid! (5) _____
e) *there* + *be* = something exists	There's a message. There aren't any tickets. (6) _____
f) *be* + *ing* = present continuous	I'm just looking. She's wearing a suit. (7) _____

*Note: To talk about age you use *be* (not *have*): **I'm** *twenty-three*. (NOT ~~I have twenty-three.~~)

Note: To talk about physical states you use *be* (not *have*): **I'm *hungry*. (NOT ~~I have hunger.~~)

2 Write your own example sentence for each use of *be*.

14 TV

Grammar Future forms: *want to, would like to, hope to, (be) going to*
Vocabulary TV programmes
Useful phrases Suggestions and offers

Vocabulary & Listening

1 Complete the questions with the words in the box.

> channels   on   programme   switch on   ~~televisions~~   watch

a) How many *televisions* do you have in your house?
b) How many hours of TV do you _____ every day?
c) When do you usually _____ the television? When do you switch it off?
d) How many different _____ can you get on your television?
e) What's your favourite TV _____ ?
f) What's _____ TV this evening?

🌐 **3.17** Listen, check and repeat.

2 Work with a partner. Ask and answer the questions in Exercise 1.

3 🌐 **3.18** Listen and number (*1–6*) the TV programmes in the order you hear them.

a game show ☐1

a documentary ☐

the news ☐

a soap opera ☐

a reality TV show ☐

a chat show ☐

Write down the names of some TV programmes in your country. What kinds of programmes are they?

Speaking

Work in small groups. Discuss the questions.

a) What programmes do you often watch / sometimes watch / never watch?
b) At the moment, which programme(s) do you really like / really hate?
c) Which TV channel has the best programmes / the worst programmes?

Reading

Eddie

Lynne

Sheryl

Josh

Adam

Tonya

1 🔵 **3.19 Read the *Big Brother* web page and answer the questions.**

a) What kind of person do they want on *Big Brother*?
b) What happens on *Big Brother*?
c) How much can you win?

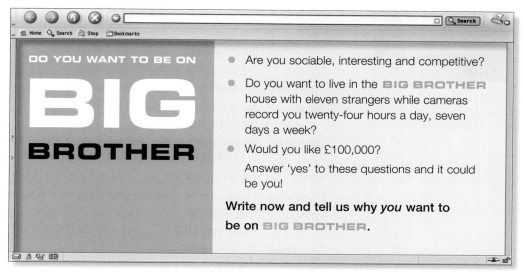

2 🔵 **3.20 Listen and read. Match the people (*a–f*) with the reasons (*1–6*) they give to be on *Big Brother*.**

| a | 1 | 'I hope to win the *Big Brother* prize because my sister is in hospital. I want to pay for her operation.'

☐ 2 'One day, I hope to be a famous pop star. I want to go on *Big Brother* because millions of people watch it.'

☐ 3 'I hope to win the money and spend it all on clothes, make-up and jewellery.'

☐ 4 'I want to save the planet! I'd like to win the money and give it to Greenpeace.'

☐ 5 'I'd like to meet new people and have a good time. Oh, and I want to buy my mum a house.'

☐ 6 'I want to go on *Big Brother* because I'm really good-looking. The camera loves me!'

Discuss with a partner. Which contestant gives the best reason? Who gives the worst reason?

Grammar

1 Look again at the contestants' reasons above. <u>Underline</u> the verb structures *hope, want* and *'d like* (*would like*).

a) Do these verb structures refer to the past or the future?
b) Are *hope, want* and *'d like* followed by the infinitive with *to* or the infinitive without *to*?

2 Put the words in the correct order.

a) I / travel / to / around the world / want   *I want to travel around the world.*
b) want / live / to / in a foreign country / I
c) to / I / get married / want / don't
d) lots of children / like / have / I'd / to
e) be famous / to / wouldn't / I / like
f) hope / before I'm sixty / I / retire / to

🔵 **3.21 Listen, check and repeat.**

Tick (✓) the sentences that are true for you. Compare with a partner.

Listening & Reading

1 🔘 3.22 **Read and listen to an interview with Lynne, the winner of** *Big Brother*. **She's talking about her future plans. What job would she like to do?**

Lynne

Interviewer: Lynne, congratulations!

Lynne: Thank you. I can't believe it.

Interviewer: What's the first thing (1) *you're going to* do when you leave the *Big Brother* house?

Lynne: (2) _____ have a big party. I missed my friends so much.

Interviewer: Ah. What (3) _____ do with the money?

Lynne: (4) _____ buy a house for my mum.

Interviewer: Oh, that's great. Which *Big Brother* housemates (5) _____ see again?

Lynne: There are some people I'd like to see again, but (6) _____ see Sheryl and Josh – they were horrible to me.

Interviewer: Oh yes, that's true ... But what about Eddie? You became really good – er – friends in the house. (7) _____ see Eddie again?

Lynne: Yes, of course (8) _____ see one another. I really miss him.

Interviewer: Finally, Lynne, what are your plans for the future?

Lynne: Well, first (9) _____ go out and spend some money. Then I want to start my singing career. (10) _____ record a CD. I'd also like to be an interviewer on TV.

Interviewer: Oh, well, good luck!

2 **Complete the conversation in Exercise 1 with the phrases in the box. You can use the phrases more than once.**

> are you going to I'm going to I'm not going to we're going to you're going to

Listen again and check your answers.

Grammar

(be) going to

I'm
You're
He's
She's **going to**
It's
work.
We're
They're

be.
come.

Are you **going to come?**
Yes, I **am.**
No, I'**m not.**

1 **Complete the questions and answers about Lynne's future plans and intentions.**

a) '*Is she* going to have a big party?' 'Yes, *she is.*' 'No, *she isn't.*'

b) '_____ she going to buy a house for her mum?' 'Yes, she _____.' 'No, she _____.'

c) '_____ going to see Sheryl and Josh?' 'Yes, _____.' 'No, _____.'

d) '_____ to see Eddie?' '_____.' '_____.'

e) '_____ go out and spend some money?' '_____.' '_____.'

f) '_____ record a CD?' '_____.' '_____.'

🔘 3.23 **Listen, check and repeat.**

2 **Work with a partner. Ask and answer the questions in Exercise 1.**

3 **Rewrite these good intentions with the missing word in the correct place.**

a) I'm going do more exercise. (to) *I'm going to do more exercise.*

b) I going to eat healthier food. ('m)

c) I going to save more money. ('m)

d) I'm going spend more time with my family. (to)

e) I not going to watch so much TV. ('m)

f) I'm going to arrive late for appointments. (not)

🔘 3.24 **Listen, check and repeat.**

4 **Which of the good intentions in Exercise 3 do you have? Discuss with a partner.**

5 ▓ Grammar *Extra* 14 page 132. Read the explanation and do the exercises.

Speaking

1 Ask your partner questions about their future plans and intentions.

Question		Answer
What are you going to do	after the lesson? this evening? tomorrow? next weekend? next summer?	*I'm going to …* *I don't know.*

> What are you going to do after the lesson?

> I'm going to meet my friend for a drink.

2 Pairwork **Student A:** page 120 **Student B:** page 125

Pronunciation

1 🔊 3.25 Listen and repeat the chants. What is the missing word? How do you pronounce it in the chants?

A

What do you want _____ do?

Where do you want _____ go?

Who do you want _____ see?

I don't want _____ come.

B

What are you going _____ do?

Where are you going _____ go?

Who are you going _____ see?

I'm not going _____ come.

2 Underline the stressed words in Exercise 1. Practise the chants.

Speaking: anecdote

1 🔊 3.26 Listen to Juliet talking about her favourite TV programme. Underline the correct information.

a) 'What's your favourite TV programme?' 'It's _Desperate Housewives_ / _Who wants to be a Millionaire?_'

b) 'What sort of programme is it?' 'It's **a quiz show** / **a comedy drama**.'

c) 'Who are the main characters?' 'The main characters are **five women** / **a presenter and contestants**.'

d) 'What's it about?' 'It's about **general knowledge** / **the five women's lives**.'

e) 'Who's your favourite character?' 'I like **Bree** / **the presenter**.'

f) 'What day is it on?' 'It's on **Wednesdays** / **Thursdays**.'

g) 'What happened the last time you watched?' 'A **man won £500,000** / **Bree met a new man**.'

h) 'Why do you like it?' 'I like **the humour** / **answering the questions**.'

2 You're going to tell your partner about your favourite TV programme.

- Ask yourself the questions in Exercise 1.
- Think about *what* to say and *how* to say it.
- Tell your partner about your favourite TV programme.

> My favourite TV programme is …

Useful phrases

1 🌐 **3.27 Read and listen to the conversation. Who wants to watch *Pirates of the Caribbean*?**

Ruby: What's on television tonight?

Joe: Nothing.

Ruby: Shall we go out?

Joe: Good idea. (1) _____ go to the cinema.

Ruby: (2) _____ . What's on?

Joe: I don't know.

Ruby: Just a minute – I'll look on the internet. ... Oh great. *Pirates of the Caribbean*.

Joe: What, again? It's so old.

Ruby: Shall I book tickets?

Joe: (3) _____ . I don't want to see it again. Let's get a DVD.

Ruby: OK. (4) _____ choose a DVD?

Joe: It's OK – I'll choose. I'd like to see a film without Johnny Depp in it.

2 **Complete the conversation with the words in the box.**

> OK   Let's   Shall I   No

Listen and check.

3 **Complete the table with phrases from the conversation in Exercise 1.**

Make a suggestion	Agree	Offer to do something	Disagree
Shall we …	*Good idea.*	*I'll …*	*It's OK.*

4 🌐 **3.28 Listen and repeat the useful phrases.**

a) Shall we go out?
b) Good idea.
c) Let's go to the cinema.
d) I'll look on the internet.
e) Shall I book tickets?
f) It's OK – I'll choose.

5 **Practise the conversation. Change the name of the film and the actor.**

Vocabulary *Extra*

Television

1 Match the pictures with the types of programme.

 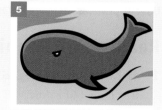 

- **9** a car<u>toon</u>
- ☐ a chat show
- ☐ a doc<u>umen</u>tary
- ☐ a game show
- ☐ the news
- ☐ a re<u>a</u>lity <u>TV</u> show
- ☐ a <u>soap</u> opera
- ☐ a <u>sports</u> <u>pro</u>gramme
- ☐ the <u>weath</u>er

2 Work with a partner. Cover the words and look at the pictures. Ask and answer questions.

> What's number 9?

> A cartoon. What's number 2?

Focus on *What ...?* and *How ...?*

1 Complete the table with the questions in the box.

> How do you do   How far is it   How much was it   What do you do   ~~What's it made of~~
> What time does it open

Some uses of *What?* and *How?*	Examples
a) *What* + verb phrase	'What do you think of Brad Pitt?' 'He's fantastic.' '(1) *What's it made of*?' 'Leather.' '(2) _____ ?' 'I'm a waiter.'
b) *What* + noun	'What colour are her eyes?' 'Blue.' 'What kind of car do you have?' 'A Peugeot.' '(3) _____ ?' '3.00 p.m.'
c) *How* + verb phrase	'How are you?' 'Fine, thanks.' 'How do you say *Italia* in English?' 'Italy.' '(4) _____ ?' 'How do you do?'
d) *How* + *much / many*	'How many people were there?' 'Eight or nine.' '(5) _____ ?' '$50'.
e) *How* + adjective / adverb	'How often do you go swimming?' 'Once a week.' 'How old are you?' '32.' 'How long did you stay?' 'About an hour.' '(6) _____ ?' 'About ten kilometres.'

2 Write your own example question and answer for each use of *What ...?* and *How ...?*

15 Experiences

Grammar Present perfect + *ever*. Present perfect or past simple?
Vocabulary Past participles
Useful phrases In a restaurant

Reading & Listening

1 🌐 **3.29 Read the magazine letter and answer the questions.**

a) How old is *International Travel Magazine*?
b) Who chose the fifteen great places to visit?
c) Who wrote the letter?

▲ Petra, Jordan

> Dear travellers,
>
> **International Travel Magazine** is fifteen years old!
> And to celebrate our fifteenth birthday, we've written a list of fifteen great places to visit.
>
> How did we choose them? We asked our colleagues here at International Travel Magazine, of course – they are all experienced travellers.
>
> We hope you enjoy our list. What are your places of a lifetime? Write to us and we'll include your places on our website.
>
> Happy travelling. Don't forget to send us a postcard!
>
> *Janet Dean (Editor)*

2 🌐 **3.30 Listen to three people who work for *International Travel Magazine*. Which places have they been to? Write *S* for Steve, *B* for Ben and *R* for Rose in the boxes in the list.**

Steve, Ben and Rose

▼ Hong Kong, China

Fifteen
places of a lifetime

Urban places
Hong Kong, China ☐ *S*
Istanbul, Turkey ☐
Rio de Janeiro, Brazil ☐

Rural places
The Loire Valley, France ☐
The North Island, New Zealand ☐
Tuscany, Italy ☐

Wild places
The Amazon, South America ☐
The Grand Canyon, USA ☐
The Sahara, Africa ☐

Islands
The Seychelles ☐
Hawaii, USA ☐
The Greek Islands ☐

Wonders of the world
Petra, Jordan ☐ *R*
Angkor Wat, Cambodia ☐
The Great Wall of China ☐

3 🌐 **3.31 Listen and repeat the fifteen places of a lifetime. Choose your top five places. Compare your choices with a partner.**

Grammar

Present perfect

I've
You've
He's
She's   **been** to Petra.
It's
We've
They've

(I've = I **have**
He's = He **has**)

Have you ever **been
to** Petra?
Yes, I **have.**
No, I **haven't.**

(**ever** = at any time up to
now)

1   If someone says 'I've been to Hawaii' what does this mean? Answer the questions.

   a)   Is the person in Hawaii now?
   b)   Did the person go to Hawaii at some time in their life 'up to now'?
   c)   Do we know *when* the person went to Hawaii?

2   Complete the table with *'s, 've, haven't* or *hasn't*.

	Affirmative	Negative
I, you, we, they	a) I ____ been to Tuscany.	b) I ____ been to Istanbul.
he, she, it	c) He ____ been to Hawaii.	d) He ____ been to Petra.

🔵 **3.32** Listen, check and repeat.

What's the full form of *I've* **and** *He's***?**

3   Complete the questions and answers.

   a)   '*Have* you ever been to Angkor Wat?'   'Yes, *I have.*'   'No, *I haven't.*'
   b)   '*Has* your father ever been to London?'   'Yes, he ____ .'   'No, he ____ .'
   c)   '____ you ever been to a big pop concert?'   '____ .'   '____ .'
   d)   '____ your mother ever been to a football match?'   '____ .'   '____ .'
   e)   '____ you and your family ever been to Paris?'   '____ .'   '____ .'
   f)   '____ students in the class ever been to your house?'   '____ .'   '____ .'

🔵 **3.33** Listen, check and repeat.

4   Work with a partner. Ask and answer the questions in Exercise 3.

Vocabulary

1   Match the actions in the pictures (*1–6*) with the past participles in the box.

work in a bar   buy a diamond ring   do a parachute jump   meet someone famous   swim with dolphins   drive a tractor

> ☑2 bought   ☐ done   ☐ driven   ☐ met   ☐ swum   ☐ worked

🔵 **3.34** Listen, check and repeat.

2   Look again at the experiences in Exercise 1. Write down what you have/haven't done.

I've worked in a bar. I haven't bought a diamond ring.

3   Write questions and ask your partner about the same experiences.

Have you ever worked in a bar?   Yes, I have.

4   **Pairwork** **Student A:** page 120   **Student B:** page 125

Pronunciation

1 Complete the chants with a past participle from the box.

| ~~broken~~ | done | driven | flown | given | known | read | said | shaken |
| spoken | swum | taken | | | | | | |

A
break broke *broken*
speak spoke _____
do did _____
swim swam _____

B
shake shook _____
take took _____
fly flew _____
know knew _____

C
give gave _____
drive drove _____
say said _____
read read _____

2 ⊙ 3.35 Listen and repeat the chants.

Reading & Listening

1 ⊙ 3.36 Read the web page. What does *Adventure World Travel* do?

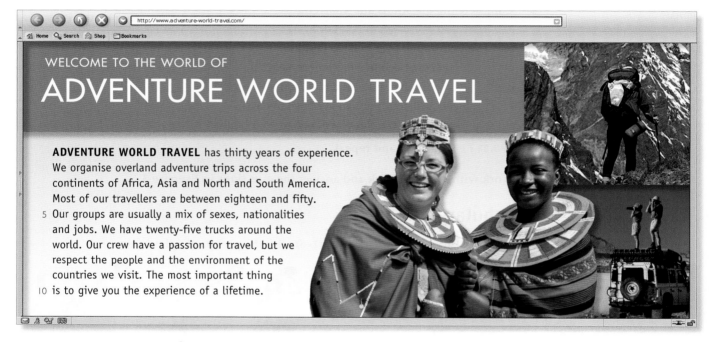

http://www.adventure-world-travel.com/

🏠 Home 🔍 Search 🛍 Shop 🔖 Bookmarks

WELCOME TO THE WORLD OF

ADVENTURE WORLD TRAVEL

ADVENTURE WORLD TRAVEL has thirty years of experience.
We organise overland adventure trips across the four
continents of Africa, Asia and North and South America.
Most of our travellers are between eighteen and fifty.
5 Our groups are usually a mix of sexes, nationalities
and jobs. We have twenty-five trucks around the
world. Our crew have a passion for travel, but we
respect the people and the environment of the
countries we visit. The most important thing
10 is to give you the experience of a lifetime.

2 Read the web page again. What do the numbers in the box refer to?

| four | eighteen and fifty | twenty-five | thirty |

Rick

3 ⊙ 3.37 Rick works for *Adventure World Travel*. Listen to him talking to his oldest friend, Will. Where is Rick phoning from?

4 Match the two sentence halves to describe Rick's experiences.

a) He's seen
b) He's driven
c) He's been
d) He hasn't had
e) He's had
f) He's met

1 a few problems with the police.
2 12,000 kilometres.
3 to Brazil.
4 lots of nice people.
5 a lot of South America.
6 any accidents.

Listen again and check your answers.

Will

5 Work with a partner. Discuss the questions.

a) What's the longest journey you've ever made?
b) What's the most interesting / adventurous holiday you've ever had?
c) What's the best place you've ever visited?

Grammar

Present perfect or past simple?

Present perfect

Completed action in 'time up to now'. (You *don't* focus on 'when'.)

Have you **been** to Brazil?
Yes, I **have**.
No, I **haven't**.

Past simple

Completed action at a specific past time. (You focus on 'when'.)

When **did** you **go**?
I **went** in February.

1 🌐 **3.38 Read and listen to part of the conversation on page 102. Answer the questions.**

Will: Have you been to Brazil?
Rick: Yeah, I have.
Will: When did you go?
Rick: In February. I went to the Carnival in Rio.
Will: Amazing!

a) What tense is the first question?
b) What tense is the second question?
c) Which tense do you use to focus on 'when' something happened?

2 **Complete the past simple questions in the table.**

Present perfect	Past simple
a) Have you ever been to Rome?	When / go? Who / go with? *When did you go? Who did you go with?*
b) Have you ever moved house?	When / move? Where / move to?
c) Have you ever lost your credit card?	When / lose it? What / do?
d) Have you ever won a prize?	What / win? When / win it?
e) Have you ever seen a Shakespeare play?	When / see it? Which one / see?

🌐 **3.39 Listen, check and repeat.**

3 **Ask your partner the questions (*a–e*) in Exercise 2. If they answer 'yes', ask the follow-up questions in the past simple.**

4 **Grammar *Extra* 15** page 132. Read the explanation and do the exercises.

Speaking: anecdote

1 🌐 **3.40 Listen to Tom talking about his oldest friend. Underline the correct information.**
a) 'What's his or her name?' 'His name is **Peter** / Simon.'
b) 'Where did you first meet?' 'We first met at **secondary school** / **university**.'
c) 'How old were you?' 'We were **six** / **thirteen or fourteen** years old.'
d) 'Why did you become friends?' '**We like the same music** / **We laugh at the same things**.'
e) 'What does your friend do now?' 'He's **a doctor** / **a teacher**.'
f) 'How often do you see him?' 'I see him **all the time** / **a few times a year**.'
g) 'When was the last time you saw him?' '**Last year** / **On his birthday**.'
h) 'What is your best memory of him?' '**A holiday we had together** / **His wedding**.'

2 **You are going to tell your partner about your oldest friend.**
• Ask yourself the questions in Exercise 1.
• Think about *what* to say and *how* to say it.
• Tell your partner about your oldest friend.

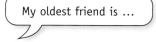

My oldest friend is ...

Useful phrases

1 Read and listen and put the parts (*a–e*) of the restaurant conversation in the correct order (*1–5*).

1 – d

a) Mrs Jones: Could we have the bill, please?
Waiter: Certainly, madam. Was everything all right with your meal?
Mrs Jones: Yes, it was lovely, thank you.

b) Waiter: Here are the menus. Would you like something to drink?
Mrs Jones: Mineral water, please.
Mr Jones: I'll have a glass of red wine.
Mrs Jones: Wine at lunchtime?
Mr Jones: Only one glass.

c) Waiter: Are you ready to order?
Mrs Jones: Yes. Two steaks, please.
Waiter: How would you like the steaks?
Mr Jones: Rare.
Mrs Jones: Medium.

d) Waiter: Good afternoon, sir. Good afternoon, madam.
Mr Jones: Good afternoon. A table for two, please.
Waiter: Certainly. Smoking or non-smoking?
Mr Jones: Non-smoking, please.

e) Waiter: Would you like to see the dessert menu?
Mr Jones: Yes, please.
Mrs Jones: No, thank you. You're on a diet, remember.
Mr Jones: Oh, yes. I'll have an es-presso, please.
Waiter: Madam?
Mrs Jones: I'll have a tea.

🌐 3.41 **Listen and check.**

2 Look at the menu. Tick (✓) the items the man and woman chose.

3 🌐 3.42 **Listen and repeat the useful phrases.**

a) A table for two, please.
b) Would you like something to drink?
c) I'll have a glass of red wine.
d) Are you ready to order?
e) Would you like to see the dessert menu?
f) Could we have the bill, please?

4 Work in groups of three. Practise the conversation. Choose differ-ent items from the menu.

Lunch menu

STARTERS

Soup of the day ☐
Prawns ☐
Liver pâté ☐

MAIN COURSES

Salmon ☐
Steak ☐
Pasta ☐

DESSERTS

Ice cream ☐
Apple pie ☐
Fruit salad ☐

DRINKS

Red wine ☐
White wine ☐
Champagne ☐
Beer ☐
Mineral water ☐
Coke ☐

HOT DRINKS

Espresso ☐
Cappuccino ☐
Tea ☐

Vocabulary *Extra*

In a restaurant

1 Match the pictures with the dishes.

- [9] apple <u>pie</u>
- [ ] <u>chick</u>en <u>sal</u>ad
- [ ] fruit <u>sal</u>ad
- [ ] ice cream
- [ ] <u>mel</u>on
- [ ] prawns
- [ ] <u>salm</u>on
- [ ] steak and chips
- [ ] to<u>ma</u>to <u>soup</u>

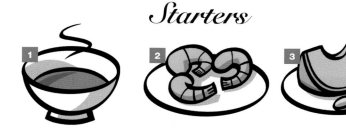

Starters

Main courses

Desserts

2 Work with a partner. Cover the sentences and look at the pictures. Ask and answer questions.

> What's number 9?

> Apple pie. What's number 5?

3 Tell your partner about your favourite meal.

Focus on verb + prepositional phrases

1 Complete the table with the verbs in the box.

arrive   ~~know~~   listen   look   talk   wait

Some common verb + prepositional phrases	Examples
a) verb + *about*	What do you (1) *know* **about** her? What did you (2) _____ **about**?
b) verb + *at*	Don't point **at** them! They're going to (3) _____ **at** the airport at 3.00 p.m. Do you want to (4) _____ **at** my holiday photos?
c) verb + *for*	How would you like to pay **for** this? Can you (5) _____ **for** me?
d) verb + *to*	I explained the situation **to** him. What sort of music do you (6) _____ **to**?

2 Write your own example sentence for each verb in Exercise 1.

16 Drive

Grammar Questions with prepositions. Tense review
Vocabulary Prepositions of movement. Places in a city / the country
Useful phrases Directions

Reading

1 🌐 **3.43 Read the article. Add the headings:** *The best drive* **and** *The worst drive.*

DRIVING TO WORK

a) _____

Jack Spencer works at the Cape Otway lighthouse. It's near the Great Ocean Road, about two hundred kilometres from Melbourne in southern Australia.

Jack lives about fifty kilometres from Cape Otway. He
5 believes that his drive to work is the most spectacular drive in the world. 'Thousands of tourists visit the Great Ocean Road every year. I'm lucky – I drive along it every day on my way to work,' he says.

Every morning, he drives to work along the coast. It
10 takes him about forty minutes. 'Traffic isn't a problem,' Jack says. 'I'm usually on the road before the tourists get up.'

He drives through rainforest and past waterfalls. As he drives through the National Park, he often sees koalas and kangaroos.
15 'From the top of my lighthouse, I have the best view in the world,' says Jack.

b) _____

Siriwan lives in the Thai capital, Bangkok, with her husband and two children.

Her office is seven kilometres from her house, but it
20 takes her two hours to get there by car in the morning. 'We have terrible traffic jams in Bangkok,' says Siriwan.

Before she goes to the office, she takes her children to school. She leaves home at 5.00 a.m. The children sleep until they arrive at school. Then Siriwan wakes them up,
25 and gives them breakfast in the car. The children go into school, and Siriwan begins her journey through the city centre, to her office.

In the evening, the traffic is worse. Cars move very slowly down Sukhumvit Road, and in the rainy season
30 it doesn't move at all. 'Everybody has a car, and there just aren't enough roads in the city,' Siriwan explains.

2 **Complete the sentences with** *He, him* **or** *his* **for Jack and** *She* **or** *her* **for Siriwan.**

a) *He* lives about fifty kilometres from *his* work.

b) _____ lives about seven kilometres from _____ work.

c) It takes _____ two hours to get to work.

d) It takes _____ forty minutes to get to work.

e) _____ goes along the coast and through the National Park.

f) _____ goes down Sukhumvit Road and through the city centre.

🌐 **3.44 Listen, check and repeat.**

3 **Write answers to these questions.**

a) How far do you live from your work/school?
b) How long does it take you to get to work/school?
c) What do (or don't) you like about your journey to work/school?

Compare your answers with a partner.

Vocabulary

Prepositions

past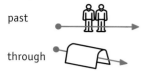

through

over

along

across

up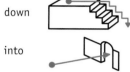

down

into

out of

1 <u>Underline</u> the correct preposition.

On my way to work / school

a) I go **down** / **through** the stairs.
b) I go **out of** / **along** my apartment.
c) I go **through** / **across** the street.
d) I go **into** / **along** the river.
e) I go **past** / **down** some shops.

f) I go **across** / **up** a hill.
g) I go **through** / **along** the park.
h) I go **up** / **over** a bridge.
i) I go **into** / **down** my office.

🔵 3.45 **Listen, check and repeat.**

2 Tick (✓) the sentences in Exercise 1 that are true for your journey to work/school.

3 Write a detailed description of a journey you often make. Use prepositions from Exercise 1.

On my way to work, I go out of my house and across the street. I go ...

Compare your description with a partner.

Grammar

1 Put the words in the correct order to make questions about a journey.

Questions with prepositions

Where do you come **from**?
What did you talk **about**?
What are you listening **to**?

a) Where / you / from / do / start ? *Where do you start from?*
b) Who / with / do / travel / you ?
c) What / talk / about / you / do ?
d) What kind of music / to / do / listen / you ?
e) What kind of scenery / do / through / go / you ?
f) What kind of buildings / go / you / past / do ?

🔵 3.46 **Listen, check and repeat.**

2 Think about a journey you make regularly. Ask your partner the questions in Exercise 1.

Pronunciation

1 🔵 3.47 **Listen and repeat the words in the box.**

past   through   turn   walk

2 Add the words in Exercise 1 to the list of words with the same vowel sound.
a) /ɑː/ car start _____
b) /ɜː/ world first _____
c) /ɔː/ fourth saw _____
d) /uː/ blue two _____

🔵 3.48 **Listen, check and repeat.**

Listening

Heinz Stücke in London in 1965

1 🌐 3.49 Listen to an interview about cyclist, Heinz Stücke. When is he going to finish his journey?

2 Answer the questions with some of the numbers in the box.

10 15 22 25 50 75 207 211 1960 1962

a) How many times has he been round the world? *10*
b) When did he start his journey?
c) How old was he?
d) How many countries has he visited?
e) How many passports has he filled?
f) How many kilos does his bike weigh?

Listen again and check.

3 What is the longest (bicycle) journey you have ever made? Tell your partner.

> The longest journey I have ever made was when I went ... I started in ...

Grammar

Tense review

Present simple:
I **drive**.

Past simple:
I **drove**.

Present continuous:
I**'m driving**.

Future with (*be*) *going to*:
I**'m going to drive**.

Present perfect:
I**'ve driven**.

1 Complete the summary of Heinz Stücke's amazing journey. <u>Underline</u> the correct tense.

The amazing Heinz Stücke

Heinz Stücke (1) **has been** / **went** round the world ten times by bicycle. He (2) **has started** / **started** his journey forty-five years ago. He (3) **has left** / **left** Germany when he (4) **is** / **was** twenty-two years old.

He (5) **has visited** / **visited** two hundred and eleven countries and he (6) **has filled** / **filled** fifteen passports.

His bicycle (7) **weighs** / **has weighed** twenty-five kilos. He usually (8) **sleeps** / is sleeping in a tent and he (9) **is making** / **makes** money by selling postcards of his trip.

At the moment, he (10) **cycles** / **is cycling** along the south coast of England.

When (11) **does he finish** / **is he going to finish** his journey? He (12) **hasn't known** / **doesn't know**. Maybe never!

🌐 3.50 Listen and check.

2 Pairwork **Student A:** page 120 **Student B:** page 125

3 Grammar *Extra* 16 page 132. Read the explanation and do the exercises.

Vocabulary

1 Look at photos of places Heinz Stücke has visited. Match each wordlist (*a–d*) with a photo (*1–4*).

a) trees, <u>forest</u>, <u>wa</u>terfall, bridge 3

b) <u>de</u>sert, sand, tree ☐

c) sea, sand, rocks, beach, cliffs ☐

d) fields, grass, hills, <u>moun</u>tains, snow ☐

🔘 **3.51** Listen, check and repeat.

2 How many things in Exercise 1 are there near your house? Put the words on a line.

my house ——— X ——————————— X ——— furthest away
            a tree   a beach

Compare with a partner.

3 Have you been to places like the ones in Heinz Stücke's photos? Would you like to? Tell your partner.

Speaking: anecdote

1 🔘 **3.52** Listen to Carla talking about the last time she went on an interesting drive. <u>Underline</u> the correct information.

a) 'When did you go for a drive?' 'I went <u>**last spring**</u> / **last weekend**.'

b) 'Where did you go?' 'I went to **Tuscany** / **the Alps**.'

c) 'Who did you go with?' 'I went with **my family** / **my friend**.'

d) 'What kind of car were you in?' 'We were in **a Mini** / **a Mazda**.'

e) 'What time did you leave?' 'We left **at night** / **in the morning**.'

f) 'What was the weather like?' 'It was **sunny** / **raining**.'

g) 'What sort of places did you drive through?' '**Green fields and hills** / **Mountains**.'

h) 'Where did you stop?' 'We stopped **in a village** / **at a motorway café**.'

i) 'What time did you arrive?' 'We arrived **in the morning** / **in the afternoon**.'

2 You are going to tell your partner about the last time you went on an interesting drive.

• Ask yourself the questions in Exercise 1.

• Think about *what* to say and *how* to say it.

• Tell your partner about your drive.

> Last … I went to …

Useful phrases

1 Match the pictures (*1–8*) with the useful phrases.

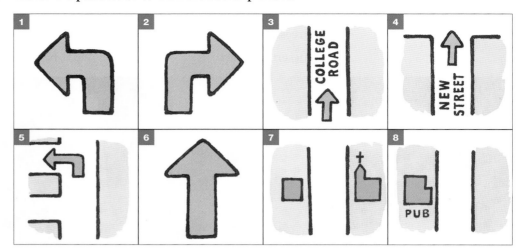

[3] Go down College Road.

☐ Opposite the church.

☐ Take the second turning on the left.

☐ Go straight on.

☐ There's a pub on the left.

☐ Go to the end of New Street.

☐ Turn right.

☐ Turn left.

🌐 **3.53 Listen, check and repeat.**

2 🌐 **3.54 Listen to three phone conversations (*a–c*) and look at the map. Write the number (*1–3*) of the destination in each case.**

3 Complete the conversation with directions from the roundabout to destination 4.

A: Hi, I'm at the roundabout.
B: OK. Go (1) *down* London Road and (2) _____ the first turning on the right. That's Victoria Street.
A: OK.
B: OK. Take the first (3) _____ on the left.
A: OK.
B: Then go to the (4) _____ of Cricket Road and (5) _____ right. There's a cinema (6) _____ the left, and our house is (7) _____ .
A: OK. Great. See you soon.

🌐 **3.55 Listen, check and repeat.**

4 Work with a partner. Write a similar conversation with directions from the school to a place that you know.

Practise your conversation.

Vocabulary *Extra*

Nature

1 Match the pictures with the nature words.

- [5] a beach
- [ ] a cliff
- [ ] a <u>de</u>sert
- [ ] a field
- [ ] a <u>fo</u>rest
- [ ] grass
- [ ] hills
- [ ] a <u>moun</u>tain
- [ ] a rock
- [ ] sand
- [ ] a tree
- [ ] a <u>wa</u>terfall

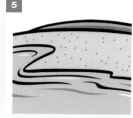

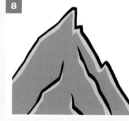

2 Work with a partner. Cover the words and look at the pictures. Ask and answer questions.

> What's number 8?

> A mountain. What's number 4?

Focus on prepositions of movement

1 Match the pictures with the prepositional phrases.

- [3] **across** the street
- [ ] **along** the river
- [ ] **down** the stairs
- [ ] **into** the building
- [ ] **out of** the house
- [ ] **past** the shops
- [ ] **through** the park
- [ ] **up** the hill

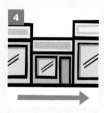

2 Work with a partner. Write another phrase for each preposition.

across the bridge

Review D

Grammar

▶ **Grammar *Extra* pages 132 and 133**

1 Put the words in the correct order to make questions.

a) you / swim / can ? *Can you swim?*
b) ski / can / you ?
c) you / can / the guitar / play ?
d) a motorbike / you / ride / can ?
e) drive / a bus / can / you ?
f) you / three languages / can / speak ?

Work with a partner. Ask and answer the questions.
'Can you swim?' 'Yes, I can. / No, I can't.'

2 Write the adverbs.

a) bad *badly*   c) fast   e) happy   g) quiet
b) careful   d) good   f) loud   h) slow

3 Complete the sentences with an adverb from Exercise 2 to make the sentences true for you. Try to use a different adverb for each sentence.

a) I usually drive my car *slowly*.
b) I always do my homework _____ .
c) I play football _____ .
d) I cook _____ .
e) I usually read books _____ .
f) I like to play my music _____ .

Work with a partner. Make questions. Ask and answer the questions with your partner.

'Do you usually drive your car slowly?'
'Yes, I do.' / 'No, I don't. I usually drive fast.'

4 Change the frequency expressions in *italics* to make the sentences true for you. Tick (✓) the sentences that are already true.

a) I travel to another country *twice a year*.
   I travel to another country **once a year**.
b) I go to the dentist *four times a year*.
c) I see my doctor *every two years*.
d) I buy a new car *every five years*.
e) I brush my teeth *twice a day*.
f) I buy a newspaper *once a week*.

Compare your sentences with a partner.

5 Complete the text with the words in the box.

~~going to~~ hope like to want to wouldn't like to

Next year I'm (1) *going to* travel to Thailand. When I'm there I (2) _____ to do some scuba diving. But I don't (3) _____ spend all my time in the sea. I'd (4) _____ go shopping in Bangkok. I love Bangkok, but I (5) _____ live there – it's too hot !

Work with a partner. Tell each other your plans for your next holiday.

6 Complete the conversation.

Tom: (1) *Have* you ever been to a rock concert?
Jane: Yes, I (2) _____ .
Tom: When (3) _____ you go?
Jane: I (4) _____ last July.
Tom: (5) _____ you ever been to the USA?
Jane: No, I (6) _____ .

Work with a partner. Ask and answer questions about these places: *South America, a music festival, a sports tournament, Egypt, Rome.*

7 Complete with the verbs in the correct tense.

Hi Dad

I (1 sit) 'm sitting here in a small café in Tokyo. I (2 eat) _____ noodle soup. Delicious! The weather (3 be) _____ really good, and the people (4 be) _____ friendly and helpful.
  I (5 arrive) _____ here yesterday morning. Before that I (6 be) _____ in Vietnam. This evening I (7 see) _____ Yuko, a very good friend. She (8 live) _____ here in Tokyo. She (9 work) _____ for Sony.
  I (10 visit) _____ a lot of places in my life, but this is the first time I (11 go) _____ to Asia. I (12 love) _____ it!

Lots of love, Andy

8 Spot the mistake! Cross out the incorrect sentence, *a* or *b*.

1 a) He can speak three languages.
   b) ~~He can to speak three languages.~~
2 a) I play very well football.
   b) I play football very well.
3 a) Where do you come from?
   b) Where do you from?
4 a) Have he ever been to Dubai?
   b) Has he ever been to Dubai?
5 a) She's going to meet us later.
   b) She's going meet us later.
6 a) What are you listening?
   b) What are you listening to?

Vocabulary

1 <u>Underline</u> the correct word.

a) Tom is very sure of himself. He's really **generous** / <u>**confident**</u>.

b) Carly's very **serious** / **sensible**. She never does stupid things, but she enjoys a good laugh.

c) Alan's nervous about meeting my parents. He's very **shy** / **selfish**.

d) Olly's so **confident** / **generous**. He buys presents for everybody.

e) Katy never thinks about other people – she's so **selfish** / **sensible**.

f) Rona's very **serious** / **shy**. She thinks about things a lot and she never smiles.

Work with a partner. Choose two adjectives to describe your partner. Ask your partner to guess which adjectives you chose.

2 Match each description with the name of a type of TV programme in the box.

> chat show   documentary   ~~game show~~   news
> reality TV show   soap opera

a) People play games and win money. *game show*

b) You find out what's happened recently in the world.

c) Famous people talk about themselves.

d) You can learn facts about people, history or nature.

e) This is a daily drama about the lives of a group of characters.

f) Ordinary people, not actors, are the stars of this type of show.

Work with a partner. Discuss your favourite type of TV programme.

3 Write the past participles of the verbs in the box.

> ~~buy~~   eat   go   meet   read   swim

buy – bought

4 Complete the questions with past participles from Exercise 3.

a) What's the most expensive thing you've ever *bought*?

b) Have you ever _____ in a fast food restaurant?

c) What's the best book you've ever _____ ?

d) Have you ever _____ to Australia?

e) Who's the most interesting person you've ever _____ ?

f) Have you ever _____ in a lake?

Work with a partner. Ask and answer the questions.

5 <u>Underline</u> the correct prepositions.

I needed some air. I ran (1) **across** / <u>**down**</u> the stairs and (2) **out of** / **up** the apartment. I didn't know what I was doing. I went (3) **across** / **past** the street and started walking. I didn't stop until I came to the river. I walked (4) **along** / **through** the river for a little while. I went (5) **into** / **past** some people but I didn't speak to them. I came to a bridge and went (6) **out of** / **over** it to the other side of the river. There was a park. I walked (7) **down** / **through** the park and, slowly, started to feel better. I went home. I went (8) **along** / **into** my apartment and walked (9) **out of** / **up** the stairs. I sat down and fell asleep. When I woke up, I didn't know if it was all a dream, or not.

6 Complete the nature words with *a, e, i, o, u*.

a) be*a*ch
b) cliff
c) d__s__rt
d) f__ __ld
e) f__r__st
f) gr__ss
g) h__ll
h) m__ __ntain
i) r__ck
j) s__nd
k) sn__w
l) w__t__rf__ll

How many of the words can you find in the photo?

forest, …

Pronunciation

1 Look at some words from Units 13–16. Say the words and add them to the table.

> ~~adventure~~   appointment   ~~carefully~~   ~~channel~~
> ~~competitive~~   desert   ~~dessert~~   experience
> generous   koala   respect   selfish   sensible
> spectacular   weekend

A: ☐□	B: ☐□□	C: □☐
channel	*carefully*	*des**se**rt*

D: □☐□□	E: □☐□□
*ad**ven**ture*	*compe**ti**tive*

2 <u>Underline</u> the stressed syllable.

🔊 **3.56** Listen, check and repeat.

Reading & Listening

1 🌐 **3.57 Read the article about Jasmine Smith. What is the name of the organisation she has started?**

An amazing woman

She worked for twenty years as a teacher. She can play the piano and guitar. She's travelled around the world and visited forty-five countries on her own. What's
5 so special about that? Well, nothing, except she can't see. Jasmine Smith is blind. She's been blind all her life.

Jasmine's parents didn't want her to go to a special school, so they sent her
10 to the local secondary school. She was a good student and she went to college. After college she became a teacher at a school for blind children. But last June Jasmine left her job after twenty years
15 and started the organisation *Blind Hope*. 'I've helped a lot of blind children in this country, but now I want to do something for blind children in other countries,' says Jasmine.
20 Does Jasmine have any other plans? 'Yes,' she laughs. 'I'd like to climb Mount Kilimanjaro and write a book.' How will she find the time? 'No problem. I never sleep at night! I'm always too busy
25 thinking of new ideas and plans,' explains Jasmine.

2 **Read the article again. Are the sentences true or false? Correct the false sentences.**

a) Jasmine was a teacher. *True*
b) Jasmine has travelled to fifty-five countries.
c) Jasmine went to a special school for blind children.
d) Jasmine taught blind children.
e) Jasmine would like to help blind children in other countries.
f) Jasmine thinks of new plans when she's working.

3 🌐 **3.58 Listen to a conversation between Jasmine and a journalist. Tick (✓) the true statement.**

a) Jasmine gave $1 million to *Blind Hope*.
b) A film star is going to Kenya.
c) A film star gave $1 million to *Blind Hope*.

4 **Listen again and <u>underline</u> the correct information.**

a) Jasmine's **<u>husband</u>** / **father**, John, helped her start *Blind Hope*.
b) Something **fantastic** / **terrible** happened two weeks ago.
c) *Blind Hope* is going to use some of the money to open a **school** / **hospital** in Kenya.
d) Jasmine is looking for **ten** / **twelve** people to help her.
e) The trip to Kenya is going to be **a serious job** / **a holiday**.
f) *Blind Hope* wants to build one school every **month** / **year**.

Writing & Speaking

1 Read the email. Find a mistake in each line and correct it. Check for: grammar mistakes; spelling mistakes; missing words.

Dear Jasmine

① Do you remeber me? I was in your class at Willsby
Secondary School. I heared the radio programme about you and
Blind Hope. I'd really like to help you organisation.

② What I do after school? Well, I became a firefighter. Then I
got married Linda Booker. Do you remember her? She was in
Mr Davis's class. We moved to Grimsby and had two child, a
boy and a girl. Anyway, we got divorced four year ago and I
move back to Purley.

③ Now, I'm doing something diffrent. I'm not a firefighter,
I'm a baker! I start my own business making bread and cakes.
Yes, I know I was a terrible cook at school, but I can to cook
really good now!

④ I've also travelled a lot. I love it! I been to fifteen countries
and I've done a lot work with children.

⑤ I would really like go to Kenya with *Blind Hope*.
You think I could help? I've done some building work before.
I very strong, I love children, and I make great cakes!

Best wishes,
Luigi Salvoni

2 Match the headings to the paragraphs (*1–5*) in the email.

a) His life now *Paragraph 3*
b) What he did after school
c) What he would like to do next
d) Introduction and the reason he's writing
e) His travel and other experiences

3 Tell your partner about yourself.

Say …
* what you did after (primary) school / university
* what interesting experiences you have had (travel, jobs)
* what your life is like now
* what you would like to do next

4 Write an email to an old friend about what you did after (primary) school / university, your experiences, your life now and what you would like to do next.

Exchange emails with a partner. Check your partner's work for: grammar mistakes; spelling mistakes; missing words.

🎵 **3.59 Song:** *Get Here*

Pairwork: Student A

Unit 1 Ask Student B for the missing flight numbers and complete the table.

What number is the flight from Milan?

Scheduled time	Airline	Flight number	From	Status
08:50	British Airways	(1) _____	MILAN	LANDED 08:59
09:00	American Airlines	AA132	NEW YORK	EXPECTED 12:23
09:35	Alitalia	(2) _____	ROME	LANDED 09:12
09:45	Aeroflot	SU243	MOSCOW	LANDED 09:22
10:00	Iberia	(3) _____	SEVILLE	LANDED 10:10
10:20	Air France	AF1370	PARIS	DELAYED

Unit 2 Imagine you are the woman in the photo. Invent personal details and complete Profile A.

Dateline PROFILE

Profile A

First name: _____
Surname: _____
Country: _____
Age: _____
Job: _____
Email address: _____
Home phone number: _____
Mobile phone number: _____
Favourite music: _____
Favourite sport: _____
Favourite actor: _____

Dateline PROFILE

Profile B

First name: _____
Surname: _____
Country: _____
Age: _____
Job: _____
Email address: _____
Home phone number: _____
Mobile phone number: _____
Favourite music: _____
Favourite sport: _____
Favourite actor: _____

Ask Student B questions and complete Profile B.

What's your first name?

Karl.

Is the person in Profile A a good date for the person in Profile B? Discuss with Student B.

Unit 3 Look at the family tree. Write descriptions of the people (a–e). Write three sentences for each person.

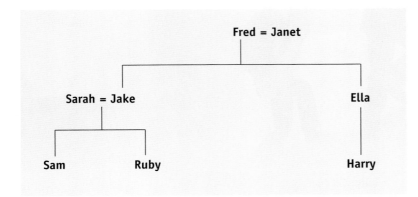

Fred = Janet

Sarah = Jake   Ella

Sam   Ruby   Harry

a) Ella *Fred and Janet are her parents …*
b) Sam and Ruby
c) Fred
d) Jake and Sarah
e) Ruby

**Read your descriptions to Student B.
Student B identifies the people.**

Student A: Fred and Janet are her parents. Jake is her brother. She has one son. Who is she?

Student B: Ella?

Student A: Yes, that's right.

Unit 4 What do you know about Student B's likes and dislikes?

Write Student B's name in the space below. Complete the sentences (a–f) with phrases from the box.
Write questions to check your sentences. Ask Student B the questions to find out if you are right or wrong.

loves   likes   doesn't like   hates

I think _____ (Student B's name) ...	Questions	✓ = I'm right! ✗ = I'm wrong!
a) *likes* going to nightclubs.	*Do you like going to nightclubs?*	✓
b) _____ swimming in the sea.	_____	_____
c) _____ eating out in restaurants.	_____	_____
d) _____ wearing sunglasses.	_____	_____
e) _____ listening to classical music.	_____	_____
f) _____ shopping for food.	_____	_____

Unit 5 It's twelve o'clock midday in London. Complete the other times.

Ask Student B questions and draw the clocks.

> What time is it in Los Angeles?

> It's four o'clock in the morning.

-11		-6		0	+1		+7	
a.m.	a.m.	a.m.	a.m.	p.m.	p.m.	p.m.	p.m.	p.m.
Honolulu	Los Angeles	Mexico City	São Paulo	London	Berlin	Moscow	Hong Kong	Sydney

Choose another time for London. Ask Student B what time it is in other cities.

> It's half past three in the afternoon in London. What time is it in Hong Kong?

Unit 6 Complete the *Me* column with an adverb to make the sentences true for your night time.

Ask Student B questions and write their answers in the *Student B* column.
Compare your answers. Are you the same or different?

> Do you ever read in bed?

> Yes, sometimes.

Night time Me	Student B	Same? Different?
a) I *never* read in bed.	*She sometimes reads in bed.*	*Different*
b) I _____ sleep with the windows open.	_____	_____
c) I _____ remember my dreams.	_____	_____
d) I _____ sleep more than seven hours.	_____	_____
e) I _____ wear pyjamas in bed.	_____	_____
f) I _____ sleep with the light on.	_____	_____
g) I _____ (your ideas)	_____	_____

Adverbs: always   usually   often   sometimes   hardly ever   never

Unit 7 Compare the first time you did these activities with the first time Student B did them.

Complete the questions with the past forms of the verbs (in brackets).
Write your answers in the *Me* column.
Ask Student B the questions and write their answers in the *Student B* column.
Compare your answers. Are you similar or different?

Questions	Me	Student B	Similar? Different?
a) When was the first time you (go) *went* to a wedding?	*A month ago.*	____	____
b) When was the first time you (travel) alone?	____	____	____
c) When was the first time you (use) a credit card?	____	____	____
d) When was the first time you (speak) to a foreigner?	____	____	____
e) When was the first time you (drive) a car?	____	____	____
f) When was the first time you (earn) some money?	____	____	____

Unit 8 What do you know about Student B?

Write Student B's name in the space below. Complete the sentences about Student B with a positive or negative past form of the verb (in brackets).
Ask Student B questions to check your sentences. Are you right or wrong?

I think _____ (*Student B's name*) …	Questions	✓ = I'm right! ✗ = I'm wrong!
a) (like) *didn't like* sport at school.	*Did you like sport at school?*	✗
b) (travel) to a different country last summer.	____	____
c) (pass) his/her driving test a few years ago.	____	____
d) (go) swimming yesterday.	____	____
e) (get up) early this morning	____	____
f) (buy) new shoes last weekend.	____	____

Unit 9 You and Student B have pictures of different living rooms. Don't look at Student B's picture.

Ask Student B questions to find what is similar and what is different.

Is there a sofa?

Yes, there is.

Are there any cupboards?

No, there aren't.

Look at your picture and Student B's picture. How is your living room at home similar or different?

In my living room there's a … / there isn't a … / there are some … / there aren't any …

Unit 10 Find out if you do similar things to Student B on a normal day.

Complete the questions with *much* or *many*.
Write your own answers to the questions in the *Me* column (*A lot, Not much/many, None*).
Ask Student B the questions and write their answers in the *Student B* column.
Compare your answers. Are you similar or different?

Questions	Me	Student B	Similar? Different?
In a normal day …			
a) how *many* emails do you send?	*A lot.*	*Not many.*	*Different.*
b) how _____ water do you drink?	___	___	___
c) how _____ CDs do you listen to?	___	___	___
d) how _____ shops do you go into?	___	___	___
e) how _____ money do you have in your pocket/bag?	___	___	___
f) how _____ chocolate do you eat?	___	___	___

Unit 11 Ask Student B to describe the people in picture B. Their names are: *Jason, Jane, Emma, Max* and *Mickey*. Label picture B.

> Which one is Jason?

> He's black. He has short, dark hair with blond highlights. He doesn't have a beard.

Marco   Karen   Lily   Paul   Susanna

1 _____   2 _____ 3 _____   4 _____   5 _____

Unit 12 Do you have the same opinions as Student B about the town/city where you are studying?

Complete the questions with the correct superlative form.
Write your answers to the questions in the *Me* column.
Ask Student B the questions and write their answers in the *Student B* column.
Compare your answers. Are you the same or different?

Questions	Me	Student B	Same? Different?
a) Which is (ugly) *the ugliest* building?	___	___	___
b) Which is (famous) park?	___	___	___
c) Which is (old) monument?	___	___	___
d) Which is (expensive) street?	___	___	___
e) Which is (big) supermarket?	___	___	___
f) Which is (popular) pub or bar?	___	___	___

Unit 13 Compare how often you and Student B do the following things.

Write your answers to the questions in the *Me* column.
Ask Student B the questions and write their answers in the *Student B* column.
Compare your answers. Are you similar or different?

Questions	Me	Student B	Similar? Different?
a) How often do you go on holiday?	_____	_____	_____
b) How often do you go to the dentist's?	_____	_____	_____
c) How often do you do exercise?	_____	_____	_____
d) How often do you check your emails?	_____	_____	_____
e) How often do you buy a lottery ticket?	_____	_____	_____
f) How often do you _____ (*your ideas*)?	_____	_____	_____

Unit 14 Have you got similar future plans and intentions to Student B?

Write your answers in the *Me* column with a ✓, ✗ or *?*
Ask Student B the questions and write their answers in the *Student B* column.
Compare your answers. Who plans the most?

Questions	Me	Student B	
a) Are you going to walk home after the lesson?	_____	_____	**Key**
b) Are you going to send any emails this evening?	_____	_____	
c) Are you going to have lunch at home tomorrow?	_____	_____	✓ = Yes, I am.
d) Are you going to go out on Saturday night?	_____	_____	✗ = No, I'm not.
e) Are you going to do any studying in the next few days?	_____	_____	? = I don't know.
f) Are you going to go anywhere interesting next week?	_____	_____	

Unit 15 What experiences has Student B had?

Write Student B's name in the space below. Read the experiences. <u>Underline</u> *has* or *hasn't*
according to your opinion.
Ask Student B questions to check if you are right or wrong.

I think _____ (*Student B's name*) ...	Questions	✓ = I'm right! ✗ = I'm wrong!
a) **has / hasn't** been to Rome.	*Have you been to Rome?*	✗
b) **has / hasn't** worked in a shop.	_____	_____
c) **has / hasn't** bought a DVD on the internet.	_____	_____
d) **has / hasn't** met somebody with the same name.	_____	_____
e) **has / hasn't** swum in a river.	_____	_____
f) **has / hasn't** driven a Mercedes.	_____	_____

Unit 16 Compare yourself and Student B.

<u>Underline</u> the correct verb form for each question.
Write your answers to the questions in the *Me* column.
Ask Student B the questions and write their answers in the *Student B* column.
Compare your answers. Are you similar or different?

Questions	Me	Student B	Similar? Different?
a) How often **do you go / are you going** swimming?	_____	_____	_____
b) What time **did you get up / have you got up** yesterday?	_____	_____	_____
c) What book **do you read / are you reading** at the moment?	_____	_____	_____
d) What **are you going to do / do you do** this evening?	_____	_____	_____
e) How many times **did you go / have you been** to England?	_____	_____	_____
f) What kind of music **are you liking / do you like**?	_____	_____	_____

Pairwork: Student B

Unit 1
Ask Student A for the missing flight numbers and complete the table.

> What number is the flight from New York?

Scheduled time	Airline	Flight number	From	Status
08:50	British Airways	BA561	MILAN	LANDED 08:59
09:00	American Airlines	(1) _____	NEW YORK	EXPECTED 12:23
09:35	Alitalia	AZ200	ROME	LANDED 09:12
09:45	Aeroflot	(2) _____	MOSCOW	LANDED 09:22
10:00	Iberia	IB4144	SEVILLE	LANDED 10:10
10:20	Air France	(3) _____	PARIS	DELAYED

Unit 2
Imagine you are the man in the photo. Invent personal details and complete Profile B.

Dateline PROFILE

Profile A

First name: _____
Surname: _____
Country: _____
Age: _____
Job: _____
Email address: _____
Home phone number: _____
Mobile phone number: _____
Favourite music: _____
Favourite sport: _____
Favourite actor: _____

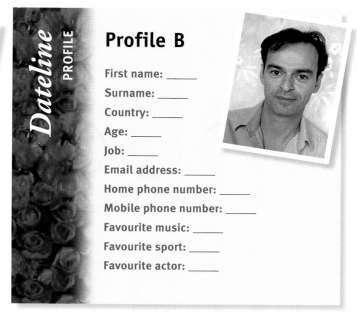

Dateline PROFILE

Profile B

First name: _____
Surname: _____
Country: _____
Age: _____
Job: _____
Email address: _____
Home phone number: _____
Mobile phone number: _____
Favourite music: _____
Favourite sport: _____
Favourite actor: _____

Ask Student A questions and complete Profile A.

> What's your first name?

> Lisa.

Is the person in Profile B a good date for the person in Profile A? Discuss with Student A.

Unit 3
Look at the family tree. Write descriptions of the people (a–e). Write three sentences for each person.

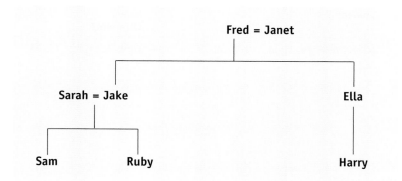

Fred = Janet

Sarah = Jake   Ella

Sam   Ruby   Harry

a) Jake   *Ella is his sister …*
b) Fred and Janet
c) Harry
d) Janet
e) Sarah

Read your descriptions to Student A.
Student A identifies the people.

Student B: Ella is his sister. Sam and Ruby are his children. Harry is his nephew. Who is he?

Student A: Jake?

Student B: Yes, that's right.

Unit 4 What do you know about Student A's likes and dislikes?

Write Student A's name in the space below. Complete the sentences (a–f) with phrases from the box.
Write questions to check your sentences. Ask Student A the questions to find out if you are right or wrong.

loves   likes   doesn't like   hates

I think _____ (Student A's name) ...	Questions	✓ = I'm right! ✗ = I'm wrong!
a) *likes* going to parties. b) _____ jogging. c) _____ eating hamburgers. d) _____ wearing jeans. e) _____ listening to jazz. f) _____ shopping for clothes.	*Do you like going to parties?* _____ _____ _____ _____ _____	✓ _____ _____ _____ _____ _____

Unit 5 It's twelve o'clock midday in London. Complete the other times.

Ask Student A questions and draw the clocks.

> What time is it in Berlin?

> It's one o'clock in the afternoon.

-11	-8		-4	0		+3		+9
a.m.	a.m.	a.m.	a.m.	p.m.	p.m.	p.m.	p.m.	p.m.
Honolulu	Los Angeles	Mexico City	São Paulo	London	Berlin	Moscow	Hong Kong	Sydney

Choose another time for London. Ask Student A what time it is in other cities.

> It's half past three in the afternoon in London. What time is it in Honolulu?

Unit 6 Complete the *Me* column with an adverb to make the sentences true for your day time.

Ask Student A questions and write their answers in the *Student A* column.
Compare your answers. Are you the same or different?

> Do you ever get up after 10.00 a.m?

> Yes, sometimes.

Day time Me	Student A	Same? Different?
a) I *never* get up after 10.00 a.m. b) I _____ have black coffee for breakfast. c) I _____ walk to work/school. d) I _____ meet friends for lunch. e) I _____ make dinner for the family. f) I _____ go to bed before midnight. g) I _____ (*your ideas*)	*He sometimes gets up after 10.00 a.m.* _____ _____ _____ _____ _____ _____	*Different* _____ _____ _____ _____ _____ _____

Adverbs: always   usually   often   sometimes   hardly ever   never

Unit 7 Compare the first time you did these activities with the first time Student A did them.

Complete the questions with the past forms of the verbs (in brackets).
Write your answers in the *Me* column.
Ask Student A the questions and write their answers in the *Student A* column.
Compare your answers. Are you similar or different?

Questions	Me	Student A	Similar? Different?
a) When was the last time you (have) *had* a haircut?	*Last week.*	____	____
b) When was the last time you (telephone) your mother?	____	____	____
c) When was the last time you (make) dinner for someone?	____	____	____
d) When was the last time you (hold) a baby?	____	____	____
e) When was the last time you (give) a present to someone?	____	____	____
f) When was the last time you (take) a photograph?	____	____	____

Unit 8 What do you know about Student A?

Write Student A's name in the space below. Complete the sentences about Student A with a positive or negative past form of the verb (in brackets).
Ask Student A questions to check your sentences. Are you right or wrong?

I think _____ (*Student A's name*) ...	Questions	✓ = I'm right! ✗ = I'm wrong!
a) (go) *went* skiing last winter.	*Did you go skiing last winter?*	✓
b) (play) a musical instrument at school.	____	____
c) (drive) to work/school this morning.	____	____
d) (watch) a good film last night.	____	____
e) (have) lunch alone yesterday	____	____
f) (visit) relatives last weekend.	____	____

Unit 9 You and Student A have pictures of different living rooms. Don't look at Student A's picture.

Ask Student A questions to find what is similar and what is different.

> Is there a sofa?

> Yes, there is.

> Are there any curtains?

> No, there aren't.

Look at your picture and Student A's picture. How is your living room at home similar or different?

> In my living room there's a ... / there isn't a ... / there are some ... / there aren't any ...

Unit 10 Find out if you do similar things to Student A on a normal day.

Complete the questions with *much* or *many*.
Write your own answers to the questions in the *Me* column (*A lot, Not much/many, None*).
Ask Student A the questions and write their answers in the *Student A* column.
Compare your answers. Are you similar or different?

Questions	Me	Student A	Similar? Different?
In a normal day …			
a) how *much* coffee do you drink?	*Not much.*	*None.*	*Different.*
b) how _____ cakes do you eat?	_____	_____	_____
c) how _____ sport do you watch on the TV?	_____	_____	_____
d) how _____ time do you spend on the internet?	_____	_____	_____
e) how _____ phone calls do you make?	_____	_____	_____
f) how _____ keys do you have in your pocket/bag?	_____	_____	_____

Unit 11 Ask Student A to describe the people in picture A. Their names are: *Lily, Marco, Paul, Karen* and *Susanna*. Label picture A.

Which one is Lily?

She has curly, blonde hair and blue eyes. She's wearing a yellow dress.

1 _____ 2 _____   3 _____   4 _____   5 _____

Jane   Emma   Mickey   Jason   Max

Unit 12 Do you have the same opinions as Student A about the town/city where you are studying?

Complete the questions with the correct superlative form.
Write your answers to the questions in the *Me* column.
Ask Student A the questions and write their answers in the *Student A* column.
Compare your answers. Are you the same or different?

Questions	Me	Student A	Same? Different?
a) Which is (interesting) *the most interesting* building?	_____	_____	_____
b) Which is (beautiful) park?	_____	_____	_____
c) Which is (modern) monument?	_____	_____	_____
d) Which is (busy) street?	_____	_____	_____
e) Which is (cheap) supermarket?	_____	_____	_____
f) Which is (quiet) pub or bar?	_____	_____	_____

Unit 13 Compare how often you and Student A do the following things.

Write your answers to the questions in the *Me* column.
Ask Student A the questions and write their answers in the *Student A* column.
Compare your answers. Are you similar or different?

Questions	Me	Student A	Similar? Different?
a) How often do you go dancing?	_____	_____	_____
b) How often do you go to the hairdresser's?	_____	_____	_____
c) How often do you do the housework?	_____	_____	_____
d) How often do you check your bank balance?	_____	_____	_____
e) How often do you buy a newspaper?	_____	_____	_____
f) How often do you _____ (*your ideas*)?	_____	_____	_____

Unit 14 Have you got similar future plans and intentions to Student A?

Write your answers in the *Me* column with a ✓, ✗ or *?*
Ask Student A the questions and write their answers in the *Student A* column.
Compare your answers. Who plans the most?

Questions	Me	Student A	
a) Are you going to drive home after the lesson?	_____	_____	**Key**
b) Are you going to cook dinner this evening?	_____	_____	
c) Are you going to have lunch in a restaurant tomorrow?	_____	_____	✓ = Yes, I am.
d) Are you going to go out on Friday night?	_____	_____	✗ = No, I'm not.
e) Are you going to do any sport in the next few days?	_____	_____	*?* = I don't know.
f) Are you going to do anything interesting next week?	_____	_____	

Unit 15 What experiences has Student A had?

Write Student A's name in the space below. Read the experiences. <u>Underline</u> *has* or *hasn't*
according to your opinion.
Ask Student A questions to check if you are right or wrong.

I think _____ (*Student A's name*) ...	Questions	✓ = I'm right! ✗ = I'm wrong!
a) <u>has</u> / **hasn't** been to Rome.	*Have you been to London?*	✗
b) **has** / **hasn't** worked in a restaurant.	_____	_____
c) **has** / **hasn't** bought a book on the internet.	_____	_____
d) **has** / **hasn't** met somebody with the same birthday.	_____	_____
e) **has** / **hasn't** swum in a lake.	_____	_____
f) **has** / **hasn't** driven a BMW.	_____	_____

Unit 16 Compare yourself and Student A.

<u>Underline</u> the correct verb form for each question.
Write your answers to the questions in the *Me* column.
Ask Student A the questions and write their answers in the *Student A* column.
Compare your answers. Are you similar or different?

Questions	Me	Student A	Similar? Different?
a) How often **do you play** / **are you playing** chess?	_____	_____	_____
b) What time **did you go** / **have you gone** to bed yesterday?	_____	_____	_____
c) What colour shoes **do you wear** / **are you wearing** at the moment?	_____	_____	_____
d) Where **are you going to have** / **do you have** dinner this evening?	_____	_____	_____
e) How many times **did you go** / **have you been** to Ireland?	_____	_____	_____
f) What kind of TV programme **are you liking** / **do you like**?	_____	_____	_____

Grammar *Extra*

Unit 1 **Nouns**

Regular forms

Singular	Plural	Spelling
a book	book**s**	Add *s*.
a toothbrush	toothbrush**es**	Add *es* after *ch*, *sh*, *s*, *x*.
a diary	diar**ies**	Add *ies* after a consonant + *y*.

Irregular forms

Singular	Plural
a person	people
a child	children
a man	men
a woman	women

⚠ *a* **or** *an*? You use *a* before a consonant sound: *a book, a key*.
You use *an* before a vowel sound: *an‿apple, an‿aspirin*.

⚠ *this* **or** *these*? You use *this* to refer to a singular noun. *'What's this?' 'It's a book.'*
You use *these* to refer to a plural noun. *'What are these?' 'They're books.'*

Unit 2 *be*: **present simple**

Affirmative	Negative	Question	Short answer Yes	Short answer No
I'm (**am**) German.	I'm **not** Polish.	**Am** I Russian?	Yes, I **am**.	No, I'm **not**.
You/We/They're (**are**) French.	You/We/They **aren't** (**are not**) Spanish.	**Are** you/we/they Italian?	Yes, you/we/they **are**.	No, you/we/they **aren't**.
He/She/It's (**is**) English.	He/She/It **isn't** (**is not**) American.	**Is** he/she/it Scottish?	Yes, he/she/it **is**.	No, he/she/it **isn't**.

In questions you put *be* before the subject: *Are you German? / Is Brad Pitt from London?* (NOT ~~You are German? / Brad Pitt is from London?~~)

Unit 3 **Possession**

Subject pronoun	I	you	he	she	it	we	they
Possessive determiner	my	your	his	her	its	our	their

You use the same possessive determiner for singular and plural. *Our family / Our friends* (NOT ~~Ours friends~~)
You use *his* for a man and *her* for a woman. *Bill and **his** wife = Bill's wife. Hillary and **her** husband = Hillary's husband.*

⚠ **Possessive *'s* or *s*'**? You use *'s* for one person. *My brother's school / My brother's friends* (= I have one brother.)
You use *s'* for more than one person. *My brothers' school / My brothers' friends* (= I have two brothers.)

Unit 4 **Present simple**

Affirmative	Negative	Question	Short answer *Yes*	Short answer *No*
I/You/We/They **work**.	I/You/We/They **don't** (**do not**) **work**.	**Do** I/you/we/they **work**?	Yes, I/you/we/they **do**.	No, I/you/we/they **don't**.
He/She/It **works**.	He/She/It **doesn't** (**does not**) **work**.	**Does** he/she/it **work**?	Yes, he/she/it **does**.	No, he/she/it **doesn't**.

In questions you put *do/does* before the subject. *Do you work in a school?* (NOT ~~You work in a school?~~)

⚠ Spelling *he/she/it* **verb endings**

Add *s* after most verbs: live – live**s**, play – play**s**, work – work**s**
Add *es* after *ch*, *sh*, *s*, *x*: watch – watch**es**, finish – finish**es**
Delete *y* and add *ies* for verbs that end in a consonant + *y*: study – stud**ies**
Irregular forms: do – **does**, go – **goes**, have – **has**

Unit 1 Exercises

1 Complete the table.

Singular	(1) *a pen*	(2) _____	a person	a baby	(5) _____	a bus	(7) _____
Plural	pens	exercises	(3) _____	(4) _____	children	(6) _____	apples

2 Write the words in the correct order.

a) It's / book / a .
   It's a book.
b) aspirin / an / It's .
c) a / woman / It's .
d) It's / watch / a .
e) umbrella / It's / an .
f) man / a / It's .

3 Rewrite the sentences in Exercise 1 in the plural.

a) *They're books.*

It's a book.   They're books.

Unit 2 Exercises

1 Write the sentences in the negative.

a) I'm from China.
   I'm not from China.
b) I'm twenty-five years old.
c) My watch is Japanese.
d) Our teacher is English.
e) My parents are on holiday.
f) The Pyramids are in Tunisia.

Tick (✓) the true sentences.

2 Make questions.

a) Your mobile phone is new.
   Is your mobile phone new?
b) Your name is Maria.
c) Your computer is an Apple.
d) You are at home.
e) Your favourite band is U2.
f) All your friends are students.

Answer the questions.

Unit 3 Exercises

1 Complete the text about Tom with *my, your, his, her, our, their*.

(1) *My* name is Tom. (2) _____ brother's name is Richard. We're English, but (3) _____ family is from France and (4) _____ surname is Durand. Richard is married and he has two children. (5) _____ names are Harry and Jemma. (6) _____ wife is an IT technician. (7) _____ job isn't very interesting, and she doesn't like (8) _____ boss. What about you? What's (9) _____ name?

Write sentences about your family with *my, your, his, her, our, their*.

2 Underline the correct form.

a) How old is your **parent's** / **parents'** house?
b) When are your **parent's** / **parents'** birthdays?
c) What is your **mother's** / **mothers'** job?
d) Who are your **mother's** / **mothers'** favourite singers?
e) What colour is your **father's** / **fathers'** car?
f) What are your **father's** / **fathers'** favourite drinks?

Ask your partner the questions.

Unit 4 Exercises

1 Complete the sentences with *I* or *My teacher*.

a) *I* live in the city centre.
b) _____ like doing housework.
c) _____ wears a watch.
d) _____ work in a shop.
e) _____ speaks French.
f) _____ has a mobile phone.
g) _____ study computer science.
h) _____ does yoga.

Write the sentences in the negative.

Tick (✓) the true sentences.

2 Write the words in the correct order.

a) Do / the guitar / play / you ?
   Do you play the guitar?
b) your friends / study / Do / English ?
c) smoke / Does / your teacher ?
d) drive / a sports car / your father / Does ?
e) you / gin and tonic / Do / drink ?
f) to the gym / Does / go / your mother ?

Answer the questions.

a) *Yes, I do.*

Unit 5 **Time**

It's **twelve** o'clock.

It's **five** past.

It's **ten** past.

It's **quarter** past.

It's **twenty** past.

It's **twenty-five** past.

It's **half** past.

It's **five** to.

It's **ten** to.

It's **quarter** to.

It's **twenty** to.

It's **twenty-five** to.

You can ask *What time is it?* or *What's the time?*

You use *It's* + time to answer the question.
***It's** six o'clock.*

You use *at* + time to say when you do something.
*I get up **at** half past seven (or seven thirty).*
*I go to bed **at** eleven fifteen (or quarter past eleven).*

Unit 6 **Adverbs of frequency**

100%   0%

| always | usually | often | sometimes | hardly ever | never |

You use adverbs of frequency before a main verb.
*I **always** have coffee for breakfast.* (NOT ~~I have always coffee …~~)
*He **doesn't usually** drink beer.* (NOT ~~He doesn't drink usually beer.~~)

⚠ *be* You use adverbs of frequency <u>after</u> *be (am / are / is)*. *She's **always** happy.* (NOT ~~She always is happy.~~)

Unit 7 **Past simple: affirmative forms**

Affirmative
I / You / He / She / It / We / They **worked, played, went, had**, etc.

There is only *one* past form for every verb (except *be*).
For regular verbs add *ed* (see below). For irregular verbs see page 143.

⚠ **Spelling regular verbs**

Add *ed* or *d* after most verbs: work – work**ed**, demonstrate – demonstrat**ed**
Delete *y* and add *ied* for verbs that end in a consonant + *y*: study – stud**ied**, try – tr**ied**
Add consonant + *ed* for verbs that end in a stressed vowel + a consonant: stop – stop**ped**, plan – plan**ned**

⚠ *be* *be* has two past simple forms: *I / he / she / it **was**   you / we / they **were***

Unit 8 **Past simple (affirmative, negative and question forms)**

Affirmative	Negative	Question	Short answer *Yes*	Short answer *No*
I / You / He / She / It / We / They **worked**.	I / You / He / She / It / We / They **didn't (did not) work**.	**Did** I / you / he / she / it / we / they **work**?	Yes, I / you / he / she / it / we / they **did**.	No, I / you / he / she / it / we / they **didn't**.

In questions you put *Did* before the subject. ***Did** you go shopping?* (NOT ~~You went shopping?~~)

⚠ *be* You don't use *Did* with *be*. *Were you at home yesterday?* (NOT ~~Did you be at home yesterday?~~)

Unit 5 Exercises

1   **What time is it? Write two ways of telling the time.**

a)   `1:05`   *It's one oh five.* / *It's five past one.*

b)   `3:15`   It's three fifteen. / _____ .

c)   `8:25`   _____ . / It's twenty-five past eight.

d)   `7:35`   _____ . / _____ .

e)   `10:45`   _____ . / _____ .

f)   `11:55`   _____ . / _____ .

2   **Write the words in the correct order**

a)   do / start school / What time / children ?
     What time do children start school?

b)   finish school / do / What time / children ?

c)   open / What time / banks / do ?

d)   What time / close / do / banks ?

e)   does / start / your English lesson / What time ?

f)   your English lesson / finish / What time / does ?

3   **Answer the questions in Exercise 2 for your town/city. Write full sentences.**

a)   *In my city, children start school at quarter to nine in the morning*

Unit 6 Exercises

1   **Write the words in the correct order.**

a)   Tom / happy / always / is
     Tom is always happy.

b)   Janet / sometimes / for breakfast / has eggs

c)   Dick / on Saturday evenings / goes out / usually

d)   Sue / tired / on Friday evenings / often / is

e)   Harry / does the housework / hardly ever

f)   Maggie / answers / her mobile phone / never

2   **Replace the names in Exercise 1 with people you know. Make true sentences.**

a)   *My grandfather is always happy.*

3   **Add adverbs of frequency to make true sentences.**

a)   I speak English in class.
     I always speak English in class.

b)   I'm late for my English lesson.

c)   I get emails in English.

d)   I speak English at work.

e)   I use English on holiday.

f)   I read magazines and books in English.

Unit 7 Exercises

1   **Complete the table for these regular verbs.**

Verb	Past simple form
a) work	*worked*
b) call	_____
c) _____	stopped
d) study	_____
e) like	_____
f) complete	_____
g) _____	tried
h) _____	listened

2   **Complete the sentences with these irregular verbs.**

a)   I (go) *went* to a party *last Saturday*.

b)   I (wear) jeans *yesterday*.

c)   I (see) a good film *two weeks ago*.

d)   I (be) very tired *last night*.

e)   I (sit) on the beach *last weekend*.

f)   I (wake up) before seven o'clock *this morning*.

3   **Change the *time expressions* to make the sentences in Exercise 2 true for you.**

Unit 8 Exercises

1   **Write sentences in the negative.**

a)   I got up late.
     I didn't get up late.

b)   I wore jeans.

c)   I did the housework.

d)   I played tennis.

e)   I had lunch with my family.

f)   I went shopping.

g)   I bought a DVD.

h)   I read the newspaper.

2   **Think about last Sunday. Tick (✓) the affirmative or negative sentences in Exercise 1 that are true for you.**

3   **Write past simple questions with *you* for the sentences in Exercise 1.**

a)   *Did you get up late last Sunday?*

4   **Ask your partner the questions in Exercise 3.**

Unit 9 *there is / there are; some/any*

	Affirmative	Negative	Question	Short answer *Yes*	Short answer *No*
Singular	**There's (is)** a sofa.	**There isn't (is not)** a carpet.	**Is there** a doctor?	Yes, **there is.**	No, **there isn't.**
Plural	**There are** some pictures.	**There aren't (are not)** any mirrors.	**Are there** any hotels?	Yes, **there are.**	No, **there aren't.**

You use *there is* or *there are* to say that something or somebody exists.

With plurals you use *some* in affirmative sentences if you don't want to give an exact number. *There are **some** people.*

With plurals you use *any* in negative sentences and questions. *There aren't **any** bars. Are there **any** hotels?*

Unit 10 **Countable and uncountable nouns**

Affirmative		
Countable nouns		**Uncountable nouns**
Singular **Plural**		some milk (NOT ~~one milk~~)
a melon two melons		some pasta (NOT ~~three pastas~~)
a grape some grapes		

Negative and question: *How many …? / How much …?*	
Countable nouns	**Uncountable nouns**
How many apples are there?	**How much** cheese is there?
There are **a lot.** ●●●●●	There's **a lot.** ▬▬▬
There are**n't many.** ●●	There isn't **much.** ▬
There aren't **any.** ○	There isn't **any.** ☐

You use *a lot (of)* in affirmative sentences. *I eat **a lot of** bread. I meet **a lot of** people.*

You use *much / many* in negative sentences and questions: *I don't drink **much** tea. I don't read **many** books. Do you eat **much / many** sweets?*

Unit 11 **Present continuous**

Affirmative	Negative	Question	Short answer *Yes*	Short answer *No*
I'm (am) working.	I'm not (am not) working.	Am I working?	Yes, I am.	No, I'm not.
You / We / They're (are) working.	You / We / They aren't (are not) working.	Are you / we / they working?	Yes, you / we / they are.	No, you / we / they aren't.
He / She / It's (is) working.	He / She / It isn't (is not) working.	Is he / she / it working?	Yes, he / she / it is.	No, he / she / it isn't.

You use the present continuous to talk about activities in progress now.

⚠ **Spelling *ing* forms**

Delete *e* and add *ing* for verbs that end in *e*: have – hav**ing**, make – mak**ing**
Add consonant + *ing* for verbs that end in a stressed vowel + a consonant: run – run**ning**, stop – stop**ping**

Unit 12 **Comparative and superlative adjectives**

	Adjective	Comparative	Superlative
Short adjectives: add *er/est*			
Adjectives ending in a consonant or *e*	old nice	old**er** nic**er**	the old**est** the nic**est**
Adjectives ending in a vowel + a consonant	big	big**ger**	the big**gest**
Adjectives ending in *y*	happy	happ**ier**	the happ**iest**
Irregular adjectives	good bad far	better worse further	the best the worst the furthest
Long adjectives: add *more / the most*	interesting	**more** interesting	**the most** interesting

You use comparative adjectives to compare people / things with other people / things. *China is **bigger than** India. Gold is **more valuable than** silver.*

You use superlative adjectives to compare people / things with all the other people / things in their group. *Russia is **the biggest** country. Platinum is **the most valuable** metal.*

Unit 9 Exercises

1 Underline the correct form.

Near my house …
a)   there are **any** / <u>**some**</u> shops.
b)   there's **a** / **any** hotel.
c)   there are **some** / **a** bars.
d)   there's **an** / **some** Italian restaurant.
e)   there's **any** / **a** park.
f)   there are **some** / **a** trees.

2 Write the sentences in Exercise 1 in the negative.

a)   … there aren't any shops.

3 Tick (✓) the sentences in Exercises 1 and 2 that are true for you.

Unit 10 Exercises

1 Make sentences with *I* and complete the table. Use *a lot of, not much* or *not many.*

	Affirmative	Negative
a) eat bread	*I eat a lot of bread.*	*I don't eat much bread.*
b) drink tea	_____	_____
c) do exercise	_____	_____
d) read books	_____	_____
e) buy magazines	_____	_____
f) get emails	_____	_____
g) meet people	_____	_____
h) have free time	_____	_____

Tick (✓) the affirmative or negative sentences that are true for you.

2 Write questions with *How much …?* or *How many …?* about the topics in Exercise 1.

a)   How much bread do you eat?

Ask your partner the questions.

Unit 11 Exercises

1 Complete the table with the verbs in the box.

| ~~come~~   ~~eat~~   ~~get~~   have   listen to   make   phone   read |
| run   sit   sleep   study   talk   use   wear   write |

Verbs ending in *e*	Verbs ending in one vowel + one consonant	All other verbs
come – coming	*get – getting*	*eat – eating*

2 Complete the holiday message.

Dear Aunty Mabel

We (1 have) *'re having* a lovely holiday in Thailand. I (2 sit) on the beach and I (3 drink) a delicious fruit juice. Joe (4 read) a book and he (5 listen) to music on his iPod. Lucy (6 swim) in the sea, and Ben (7 sleep) in the hotel. He went dancing last night. We (8 eat) a lot of good food, and I (9 get) fat!

We (10 think) of you.

Love Jenny, Joe, Lucy and Ben xxxx

Unit 12 Exercises

1 Write sentences comparing the things below. Use the adjectives (in brackets).

a)   Driving / flying (dangerous)
Driving is more dangerous than flying.
b)   French food / English food (good)
c)   Meat / fish (healthy)
d)   English / my language (difficult)
e)   Men / woman (romantic)
f)   Cats / dogs (nice)

Compare your ideas with a partner.

2 Use the prompts and write sentences about people or places you know. Use superlative forms.

a)   beach (beautiful)
The most beautiful beach I know is Ipanema beach in Rio de Janeiro.
b)   city (ugly)
c)   restaurant (expensive)
d)   person (funny)
e)   driver (bad)
f)   person (lucky)

Talk about your sentences with a partner.

Unit 13 *can*

Affirmative	Negative	Question	Short answer *Yes*	Short answer *No*
I/You/He/She/It/We/They **can swim**.	I/You/He/She/It/We/They **can't (cannot) swim**.	**Can** I/you/he/she/it/we/they **swim**?	Yes, I/you/he/she/it/we/they **can**.	No, I/you/he/she/it/we/they **can't**.

You use *can* to talk about ability. You put *can* before the subject in questions. *Can you swim?* (NOT ~~You can swim?~~)

⚠️ *can* + **infinitive without** *to* You don't use *to* after *can*. *I can swim.* (NOT ~~I can to swim.~~)

Unit 14 *(be) going to*

Affirmative	Negative	Question	Short answer *Yes*	Short answer *No*
I'm (am) going to come. You/We/They're (are) going to come. He/She/It's (is) going to come.	I'm not (am not) going to come. You/We/They aren't (are not) going to come. He/She/It isn't (is not) going to come.	Am I going to come? Are you/we/they going to come? Is he/she/it going to come?	Yes, I am. Yes, you/we/they are. Yes, he/she/it is.	No, I'm not. No, you/we/they aren't. No, he/she/it isn't.

You use *(be) going to* to talk about your future plans and intentions.

Unit 15 **Present perfect**

Affirmative	Negative	Question	Short answer *Yes*	Short answer *No*
I/You/We/They've worked. He/She/It's (has) worked.	I/You/We/They haven't (have not) worked. He/She/It hasn't (has not) worked.	Have I/you/we/they worked? Has he/she/it worked?	Yes, I/you/we/they have. Yes, he/she/it has.	No, I/you/we/they (have not) haven't. No, he/she/it hasn't.

To form the present perfect you use *have/has* + past participle. (For irregular past participles see page 143.)

You use the present perfect to talk about completed actions in 'time up to now'. You don't focus on when.
ever = at any time in your life.

⚠️ *been* *been* is the past participle of *be*, but you can also use it as a past participle of *go*. Compare the following:
1 *He's been to Rome.* = He went and came back.
2 *He's gone to Rome.* = He went and is in Rome now.

Unit 16 **Tense review**

Tense	Uses	Affirmative	Negative	Question
Present simple	Facts/habits/routines	He **works**.	He **doesn't work**.	**Does** he **work**?
Past simple	Completed action at a specific past time	She **worked** yesterday.	She **didn't work** yesterday.	**Did** she **work** yesterday?
Present continuous	Activities in progress now	They**'re working** now.	They **aren't working** now.	**Are** they **working** now?
Future *(be) going to*	Future plans and intentions	We**'re going to work** tomorrow.	We **aren't going to work** tomorrow.	**Are** we **going to work** tomorrow?
Present perfect	Completed action in 'time up to now'.	It**'s worked** recently.	It **hasn't worked** recently.	**Has** it **worked** recently?

Unit 13 **Exercises**

1   Write sentences with *can* and *can't*.

a)   I / English / not Spanish. (speak)
     I can speak English but I can't speak Spanish.
b)   I / a bicycle / not a motorbike. (ride)
c)   I / a car / not a bus. (drive)
d)   I / the guitar / not the drums. (play)
e)   I / music / not Japanese. (read)
f)   I / chess / not poker. (play)

2   Rewrite the sentences in Exercise 1 with *and* or *but* to make them all true for you.

I can speak English and I can speak Spanish (and French!).
I can't ride a bicycle and I can't ride a motorbike.

Unit 14 **Exercises**

1   Write true sentences about tomorrow with *I'm going to* or *I'm not going to*.

a)   buy a new car
     I'm not going to buy a new car tomorrow.
b)   get up early
c)   see my parents
d)   play golf
e)   watch my favourite TV programme
f)   wear jeans

2   Write questions with *you* and *your* for the sentences in Exercise 1. Then ask your partner.

a)   *Are you going to buy a new car tomorrow?*

3   Look at the picture of Jane's shopping. Write sentences about her plans for this evening.

a)   *She's going to have a pizza.*

Unit 15 **Exercises**

1   Write the sentences in the negative.

a)   I've been to New York.
     I haven't been to New York.
b)   I've seen the Pyramids in Egypt.
c)   I've driven in a foreign country.
d)   I've stayed in a five-star hotel.
e)   I've eaten sushi.
f)   I've slept on a beach.

2   Tick (✓) the affirmative or negative sentences in Exercise 1 that are true for you.

3   Write questions with *you* and *ever* for the sentences in Exercise 1.

a)   *Have you ever been to New York?*

4   Ask your partner the questions in Exercise 3. Write the answers.

a)   *Donna hasn't been to New York.*
b)   *She's ...*

Unit 16 **Exercises**

1   Name the verb tense used in the sentences.

a)   I *listen to* British and American pop songs. *Present simple*
b)   I *saw* a film in English last month.
c)   I've *written* emails in English at work.
d)   I'm *studying* for an English exam at the moment.
e)   I'm *going to do* an English language course next summer.
f)   I *like* speaking English.

2   Write the sentences in Exercise 1 in the negative.

a)   *I don't listen to British and American pop songs.*

Tick (✓) the sentences in Exercise 1 or 2 that are true for you.

Recordings

Unit 1

🔘 1.05

1	Portuguese	5	Polish
2	German	6	Spanish
3	Italian	7	Chinese
4	Russian	8	Japanese

🔘 1.06

a) 'Is he Chinese?' 'Yes, he is.'
b) 'Are they Spanish?' 'Yes, they are.'
c) 'Is it Japanese?' 'Yes, it is.'
d) 'Is she Russian?' 'Yes, she is.'
e) 'Is it Polish?' 'Yes, it is.'
f) 'Are they British?' 'Yes, they are.'

🔘 1.09

1 an aspirin, aspirins
2 an apple, apples
3 a diary, diaries
4 a toothbrush, toothbrushes

🔘 1.10

a) 'What's this?' 'It's a diary.'
b) 'What are these?' 'They're pens.'
c) 'What are these?' 'They're keys.'
d) 'What are these?' 'They're coins.'
e) 'What's this?' 'It's a bag.'
f) 'What are these?' 'They're watches.'

🔘 1.13

1	E I A U O	4	A E I O U
2	I U A O E	5	I A O U E
3	A I O E U		

🔘 1.15

a) The number for Air France is oh eight seven oh, one four two, four three four three.
b) The number for British Airways is oh eight seven oh, eight five oh, nine eight five oh.
c) The number for Lufthansa is oh eight seven oh, eight three seven, double seven four seven.
d) The number for American Airlines is zero two zero, seven three six five, zero seven double seven.
e) The number for China Airlines is zero two zero, eight seven four five, four six two four.
f) And the number for Japan Airlines is oh two oh, eight double nine oh, six oh one oh. I'll repeat that: oh two oh, eight double nine oh, six oh one oh.

🔘 1.16

(H = Helen; M = Mike)
H: Goodbye, Mike.
M: Um, can I see you in London?
H: Yes. Phone me.
M: OK. What's your surname?
H: Taylor. T–A–Y–L–O–R.
M: What's your phone number?
H: 020 7653 2001.
M: What's your email address?

H: It's helen21@hotpost.com.
M: OK, bye, Helen. See you.

Unit 2

🔘 1.21

a) I'm an actor. My favourite singers are Jimi Hendrix and Bob Marley.
b) He's the Prince of Wales. His wife is called Camilla.
c) She's from Los Angeles. Her films include *Tomb Raider* and *Mr & Mrs Smith*.
d) We're married. Our names are Bill and Hillary.
e) They're Spanish. Their surname is Iglesias.

🔘 1.23

a) thirteen   e) seventy
b) fourteen   f) eighty
c) fifty   g) nineteen
d) sixteen

🔘 1.25

In the world today …
a) 28% of people are under 15 years old.
b) 65% of people are between 15 and 64 years old.
c) 7% of people are over 65 years old.
d) 47% of people live in cities.
e) 245 people are born every 60 seconds.
f) 110 people die every 60 seconds.

🔘 1.26

a) She's nineteen.   c) She's forty-one.
b) He's sixty-four.   d) He's seven.

🔘 1.27

a) He's a lawyer.
b) She's a hairdresser.
c) They're shop assistants.
d) He's an IT technician.
e) He's a doctor.
f) He's a taxi driver.
g) He's a sales manager.
h) They're nurses.

🔘 1.28

In the UK …
a) 25% of sales managers are women.
b) 39% of doctors are women.
c) 89% of nurses are women.
d) 42% of lawyers are women.
e) 32% of IT technicians are women.
f) 83% of hairdressers are women.
g) 73% of shop assistants are women.
h) 8% of taxi drivers are women.

🔘 1.29

A: *an* with vowel sounds – an actor, an English teacher, an IT technician
B: *a* with consonant sounds – a doctor, a singer, a student, a university professor, a writer

🔘 1.30

a) George Bush is from Texas. He isn't from California.
b) Domenico Dolce and Stefano Gabbana aren't Spanish. They're Italian.
c) Isabel Allende isn't an artist. She's a writer.
d) The White House isn't in New York. It's in Washington.
e) The Petronas Towers are in Kuala Lumpur. They aren't in Hong Kong.
f) LOT is a Polish airline. It isn't a German airline.

🔘 1.31

a) 'Are you a university student?' 'Yes, I am.' 'No, I'm not.'
b) 'Are you 21?' 'Yes, I am.' 'No, I'm not.'
c) 'Is your mother a taxi driver?' 'Yes, she is.' 'No, she isn't.'
d) 'Is your father over 65 years old?' 'Yes, he is.' 'No, he isn't.'
e) 'Is your favourite drink Coke?' 'Yes, it is.' 'No, it isn't.'
f) 'Are your grandparents from here?' 'Yes, they are.' 'No, they aren't.'

🔘 1.32

a) What's your surname?
b) How old are you?
c) What's your email address?
d) What's your first name?
e) What's your mobile number?
f) What's your home phone number?
g) Where are you from?
h) What's your job?

Unit 3

🔘 1.36

a) husband and wife: Peter and Pauline
b) father and son: John and Tom
c) mother and daughter: Pat and Kitty
d) sister and brother: Jennifer and Joe
e) uncle and nephew: John and Joe
f) aunt and niece: Pat and Jennifer
g) cousin and cousin: Jennifer or Joe, and Jack
h) brother-in-law and sister-in-law: Peter and Pat

🔘 1.38

a) Peter says: 'My wife's name is Pauline.'
b) Pauline says: 'My sister's name is Pat.'
c) Joe says: `My sister's name is Jennifer.'
d) Pat says: 'My husband's name is John.'
e) Kitty says: `My brothers' names are Tom and Jack.'
f) John and Pat say : 'Our nephew's name is Joe.'

🔊 1.40

(I = Interviewer; C = Caroline;
M = Margaret)

I: Hello, Caroline. What's bad about Margaret's family?
C: The pets live in the house – ugh! Oh, and Andy and Margaret smoke in the house. That's horrible. Um, the children go to bed very late.
I: Hmm. What's good about Margaret's family?
C: Well, they do everything together. They eat meals together in the kitchen. They talk and play games together and they go out together at the weekends.
I: Thank you, Caroline. … Now, Margaret. What's bad about Caroline's family?
M: Well, Paul and Caroline work at the weekend. So the children watch TV and DVDs in their bedrooms. Ahh. And … they eat meals on the sofa in front of the TV.
I: Oh dear. What's good about Caroline's family?
M: Paul buys flowers for Caroline. That's nice. And the children go to bed early. And … the cleaner does the housework. That's very good.

🔊 1.41

a) have – has   e) live – lives
b) go – goes   f) play – plays
c) do – does   g) buy – buys
d) eat – eats   h) watch – watches

🔊 1.42

a) My parents live in a big apartment.
b) My mother goes to bed early.
c) My father buys flowers for my mother.
d) I have one sister and one brother.
e) My brother plays games on his computer.
f) My sister watches TV in her bedroom.
g) We eat meals together in the kitchen.
h) The cleaner does the housework.

🔊 1.44

a) My favourite relative is my cousin.
b) His name is Daniel, but we call him Danny.
c) He's 34 years old.
d) He lives in Los Angeles.
e) He's single.
f) He has two cats. Their names are Champagne and Caviar.
g) He's a photographer.
h) He works for *People* magazine.

Unit 4

🔊 1.49

a) 'Do you like shopping?' 'Yes, I do.' 'No, I don't.'
b) 'Does your father do the housework?' 'Yes, he does.' 'No, he doesn't.'
c) 'Do you think about chocolate all the time?' 'Yes, I do.' 'No, I don't.'
d) 'Does your mother work at the weekend?' 'Yes, she does.' 'No, she doesn't.'

e) 'Do you and your friends chat online?' 'Yes we do.' 'No, we don't.'
f) 'Do your friends go out a lot?' 'Yes they do.' 'No, they don't.'

🔊 1.50

1 I love it.   4 I don't mind it.
2 I really like it.   5 I don't like it.
3 I like it.   6 I hate it.

🔊 1.51

Jack loves water, really likes being outside and really likes sport and keeping fit. He hates towns and cities and he doesn't like loud music. He loves playing football, swimming, jogging and going to the gym. But he doesn't like shopping, clubbing, eating out in restaurants or going to rock concerts. … Oh, and he really likes Layla.

Layla loves spending money. She hates doing housework and she doesn't like cooking. She likes dancing and she doesn't mind loud music. She hates sport. She loves shopping, clubbing, eating out in restaurants and going to rock concerts. But she doesn't like playing football, swimming, jogging or going to the gym. … And Jack? She really likes him.

🔊 1.53

a) I don't like the Beatles. Do you like them?
b) I don't like Robbie Williams. Do you like him?
c) I don't like Mariah Carey. Do you like her?
d) I don't like Eminem. Do you like him?
e) I don't like the Sugababes. Do you like them?
f) I don't like pop music. Do you like it?

🔊 1.54

About me
My name's Cathy, and that's me in the photo. I'm 21, I'm a Scorpio and I'm single. I work for a big company. It's a good job, but I don't like it. I prefer being outside.
I have one brother. He's 23. I love him, but we're very different. He has a girlfriend. She's beautiful, but my parents don't like her.
We live at home with our parents. We have a sister but she doesn't live with us. She's married and she has two children. We see them all at the weekend.
I listen to all kinds of music, but my favourite is jazz. I play the saxophone, but I don't play it very well.
I'm not very sporty but I like dancing. I have lots of good friends, and I go out with them every weekend.
What about you?

Review A

🔊 1.57

(C = Customs officer; M = Man)
C: Open your bag, please, sir.
M: Yes, sure.
C: What's this?
M: It's an MP3 player.
C: Mm. And what are these?

M: They're tissues.
C: Tissues? And what's this?
M: It's a mobile phone.
C: Ah, yes. What's this?
M: It's a toothbrush.
C: Oh, … and what's this?
M: It's a camera.
C: What are these?
M: They're aspirins. I have a headache.
C: Fine. Thank you, sir.

🔊 1.58

A: cousin, husband, lawyer
B: hairdresser, manager, Portugal
C: address, Brazil, Chinese
D: assistant, computer, umbrella

🔊 1.59

(R = Rona; K = Kate)
K: Hi, Rona. It's me.
R: Oh, hi, Kate.
K: So, did you look at the website?
R: Yes, I did. Amazing!
K: And? Did you see anyone interesting?
R: Well, Ben looks nice.
K: The doctor?
R: Yes. He's tall, with dark hair, and he's very good-looking.
K: Yes, but he doesn't like football, and he doesn't like travelling.
R: Oh.
K: What about Raj?
R: Mmm. Maybe.
K: He likes eating out and travelling.
R: Yes, but he lives in London. And he likes shopping. I hate shopping, Kate!
K: Well, there's James. He lives in Glasgow too!
R: Oh … yes.
K: He's an IT technician.
R: Yeah.
K: He likes holidays, reading and football. His favourite football team is Glasgow Rangers! Go on, Rona. Call him!
R: OK. OK. Where's his number? … OK. Talk to you later. Bye. … Right, here goes. 07785 7844 532.

Unit 5

🔊 1.63

a) Nine o'clock in the morning is 9.00 a.m.
b) Six o'clock in the evening is 6.00 p.m.
c) Eleven o'clock at night is 11.00 p.m.
d) Half past six in the morning is 6.30 a.m.
e) Quarter to eight in the morning is 7.45 a.m.
f) Quarter past eight in the morning is 8.15 a.m.

🔊 1.64

a) It's 2.30. It's half past two.
b) It's 7.15. It's quarter past seven.
c) It's 1.10. It's ten past one.
d) It's 3.45. It's quarter to four.
e) It's 4.55. It's five to five.
f) It's 9.40. It's twenty to ten.

1.67

1	Monday	5	Friday
2	Tuesday	6	Saturday
3	Wednesday	7	Sunday
4	Thursday		

1.68

(I = Interviewer; T = Tanya; B = Bill; M = Mary)

I: What do you do on Saturday night?
T: I go out with my friends.
I: Where do you go?
T: We go to the cinema and then we go dancing. We drink cocktails and we have a good time.
I: What do you do on Sunday morning?
T: Sunday morning? Oh, I get up late. I don't have breakfast. I drink black coffee and read magazines.

I: What do you do on Saturday night?
B: I go to work. I'm a taxi driver.
I: Oh. Do you listen to music in your taxi?
B: Yes, I listen to the radio.
I: What do you do on Sunday morning?
B: I go home and have a shower. Then I go to bed and I sleep.

I: What do you do on Saturday night?
M: I don't go out – I stay in … with my parents.
I: What do you do with your parents?
M: We have dinner and we watch television. Then I go on the internet and chat with my friends. I go to bed late.
I: What do you do on Sunday morning?
M: We have breakfast. Then we go shopping.

1.69

a) go home, go on the internet, go out, go shopping, go to bed, go to work
b) have a good time, have a shower, have breakfast, have dinner, have lunch

Unit 6

1.74

a) do my homework, do the housework, do the shopping, do the washing, do the washing up
b) make a lot of noise, make dinner, make long phone calls, make the beds, make the decisions

1.76

a) first, second, third
b) seventh, sixth, second
c) fifth, first, fourth
d) tenth, twentieth, twelfth

1.77

Spring: March, April, May
Summer: June, July, August
Autumn: September, October, November
Winter: December, January, February

1.79

a) Something you never do on Sunday.
b) Something you always do in the morning.
c) Something you usually do at the weekend.
d) Something you always do on 31st December.
e) Something you sometimes do on Saturday night.
f) Something you usually do in the summer.

1.81

(M = Man; W = Woman)

M: Are you going to carnival this year?
W: Of course. I go every year. What about you?
M: No. I hate carnival. I'm going to the mountains for a week.
W: Really? Why?
M: I don't like all the people.
W: But it's fun. And the music is fantastic. I love it.
M: I don't like all that drumming. I like listening to music at home.
W: But what about the parades and the costumes?
M: Yes, I like the parades and costumes. I think they're great. But I like watching them on television.
W: On television?! Oh no, that's terrible. Carnival on television! I love dancing all night on the beach.

1.82

My favourite festival is Saint Patrick's Day. It takes place in Dublin, in the city centre. It takes place in March and it goes on for four days. On 17th March – the most important day – we have a big parade in the city centre. At the end of the parade, thousands of people do traditional Irish dancing together. It's fantastic. People wear green clothes and paint their faces green. We drink a lot of beer – that's Guinness of course. And we listen to traditional Irish music in the pubs. Ah, Irish people love a good party!

1.84

a) What time do you open?
b) We open at nine o'clock.
c) What time does it open?
d) What time does it close?
e) What time do you close?
f) We close at 5.30.
g) We're closed at the weekend.

Unit 7

2.02

(I = Interviewer; P = Pam; S = Sergio)

I: Excuse me. I'm from a new sports shop. Can I ask you some questions about water sports?
P: Sure.
I: Um, what's your name?
P: It's Pam.
I: OK, Pam. Do you ever go swimming?
P: Oh, yes, I love swimming.
I: And when was the last time you went swimming?
P: Er, the last time I went swimming was … in August. I was on holiday.
I: And do you ever go sailing?
P: No – I'd like to, but I don't know anybody with a boat.
I: OK, how about other water sports?
P: I sometimes go windsurfing.
I: When was the last time you went windsurfing?
P: I went windsurfing last summer with my friend. We were on holiday.
I: Great. Well, come along to our shop some time. Here's the address.
P: Yeah, thanks.

I: Excuse me. I'm from a new sports shop. Can I ask you some questions about water sports?
S: Water sports?
I: Yes, what's your name?
S: Sergio Fernandez Almira Olivera.
I: OK, er, Sergio. Do you ever go swimming?
S: Yes, yes, I go swimming a lot.
I: Oh great. When was the last time you went swimming?
S: Yesterday!
I: Right, and do you ever go sailing?
S: Yes, but not often.
I: When was the last time you went sailing?
S: I can't remember. A long time ago.
I: Do you ever do other water sports?
S: Yes, I love scuba diving.
I: Wow. When was the last time you went scuba diving?
S: Last year. I was on holiday in Egypt.
I: Lovely. Well, our new shop is in the centre of town …

2.03

a) Do you ever go swimming?
b) When was the last time you went swimming?

2.05

a) go – went, do – did, send – sent
b) hold – held, sell – sold, tell – told
c) think – thought, catch – caught, hear – heard
d) take – took, break – broke, speak – spoke
e) see – saw, come – came, wear – wore
f) read – read, say – said, give – gave

2.06

a) went, did, sent
b) held, sold, told
c) thought, caught, heard
d) took, broke, spoke
e) saw, came, wore
f) read, said, gave

2.07

A: No extra syllables: ask – asked, love – loved, stop – stopped, use – used, work – worked
B: Extra syllable: point – pointed, start – started, want – wanted

2.09

A man and woman went on holiday to the Indian Ocean. One day they went on a boat with twenty other people and went scuba diving. The boat stopped in the middle of the ocean, and everybody went diving.

After an hour everybody returned to the boat, and the boat went back to the port. But the man and woman didn't return to the boat. When they finished diving, there was no boat. At first, they shouted, but nobody heard them. They waited and waited for the boat to return, but eventually they realised they were alone.

Suddenly, something moved near them under the water.

Two or three weeks later a fisherman found their camera.

Unit 8

🌐 2.14

(I = Interviewer; N = Nelly)

I: Welcome to this week's edition of *Heroes*. Today we have the popular television presenter, Nelly B, in the studio. Nelly, hello and welcome.

N: Thank you. It's lovely to be here.

I: Nelly, who is your hero and why?

N: My hero is Debra Veal because she rowed across the Atlantic alone.

I: Alone?! That's amazing! Why did she do it?

N: Well, she started a trans-Atlantic race with her husband, Andrew. But he left after two weeks. He was frightened of the ocean.

I: Oh dear. Was she angry when Andrew left?

N: No, she wasn't angry. She was relieved when he left. She just wanted him to be happy.

I: Was it difficult for Debra to continue the journey alone?

N: Yes, it was difficult for her to sleep. She was worried about big ships. Some ships are enormous and she was in a very small boat.

I: Did she have any bad experiences?

N: Yes. She was frightened of sharks. One night there was a very big shark under the boat – but it wasn't interested in her – it was only interested in eating the fish under the boat.

I: I understand that Debra finished the race seventy days after the winners. How did she feel about that? Was she embarrassed?

N: No, she wasn't embarrassed about it. She was just happy about finishing the race.

I: Well, that's an incredible story. Nelly, thank you so much. Debra Veal is an inspiration. Next week we'll be talking to …

🌐 2.15

a) I'm worried about my future.
b) I'm never angry with my friends.
c) I'm frightened of snakes.
d) I'm not interested in modern art.
e) I'm not embarrassed about my English.

🌐 2.17

Greta Garbo was born in Sweden. She left school at fourteen and worked as a model. When she was seventeen, she went to theatre school. Soon after she moved to Hollywood and made twenty-seven films.

She didn't get married and she didn't have children. She retired when she was thirty-six. She died in New York in 1990.

🌐 2.18

a) 'Did you go to primary school near here?' 'Yes, I did.' 'No, I didn't.'
b) 'Did you walk to school?' 'Yes, I did.' 'No, I didn't.'
c) 'Did you move house when you were a child?' 'Yes, I did.' 'No, I didn't.'
d) 'Did your father leave school at sixteen?' 'Yes, he did.' 'No, he didn't.'
e) 'Did your mother study English at school?' 'Yes, she did.' 'No, she didn't.'
f) 'Did your parents go to university?' 'Yes, they did.' 'No, they didn't.'

🌐 2.19

A: feel – felt, know – knew, mean – meant, see – saw, speak – spoke, think – thought
B: break – broke, fly – flew, spell – spelt, spend – spent, teach – taught, wear – wore

🌐 2.20

felt – spelt, knew – flew, meant – spent, saw – wore, spoke – broke, thought – taught

🌐 2.21

(F = Frank; L = Lottie)

F: I don't know where to go on holiday this year. Where did you go for your last summer holiday?

L: I went to the beach – to Tarifa in the south of Spain.

F: Oh, lovely. When did you go there?

L: Um, in July.

F: Nice. Who did you go with?

L: I went alone. I always go on holiday alone.

F: Oh, right. … How did you get there?

L: I went by plane and by car. I flew from London to Malaga, and then I drove from Malaga to Tarifa. There's a really good motorway.

F: Great. Where did you stay?

L: In a hotel – the Hurricane Hotel. Do you know it?

F: No – what's it like?

L: Fantastic. The rooms are wonderful. And it's near the beach.

F: Mm, you are lucky. How long did you stay?

L: Just two weeks, unfortunately.

F: Oh, well. So what did you do all day?

L: I went to the beach, of course – you can do everything there. I tried kite surfing – it's amazing.

F: Wow – and what did you do in the evening?

L: I went out to the bars and clubs. There's a lot to do in Tarifa.

F: Mm, and did you meet anybody nice?

L: Well, yes, I did actually. He's a windsurfing instructor, and the first time we went out …

🌐 2.24

a) 'I'm bored.' 'Why don't you go out with your friends?'
b) 'I'm hungry.' 'Why don't you have a snack?'

c) 'I'm tired.' 'Me too. Let's watch a DVD tonight.'
d) 'I'm hungry.' 'Why don't you have lunch early?'
e) 'I'm thirsty.' 'Me too. Let's have a cup of coffee.'
f) 'I'm bored.' 'Why don't you play on your PlayStation?'

Review B

🌐 2.25

A: August, breakfast, frightened, nervous, Thursday
B: exercise, internet, Saturday, terrible, usually
C: embarrassed, excited, November, October, September

🌐 2.27

This is the news for Tuesday, 4th July 2006.

This morning, actor and writer, David Walliams, walked into the sea at Dover in the south of England. At 5.30 a.m. David started his swim across the English Channel. Greg Whyte, his trainer, followed him in a boat and gave him bananas and chocolate. David Walliams swam 34 kilometres from Dover to Calais in France. The swim took 10 hours and 30 minutes. The sea was cold – 15 degrees centigrade, but David didn't have any problems and arrived in Calais at 4.00 p.m. He was very happy to finish so quickly.

David made more than £1 million for the charity, Sport Relief. The money goes to help poor children all over the world.

Unit 9

🌐 2.30

Little Palm Island is exclusive. There isn't a road to the hotel: guests arrive by boat or seaplane. Come here for total peace and quiet. There aren't any phones or televisions, and there aren't any children – sixteen is the minimum age.

The Emirates Palace Hotel offers you excellent service. There are 2,600 employees – that's four for every guest in the hotel. The rooms are beautiful and well-equipped. There are 1,000 crystal chandeliers, and there's a 125-centimetre plasma TV in every room.

🌐 2.32

a) There's a bed.
b) There isn't a bookcase.
c) There are some curtains.
d) There aren't any clocks.

🌐 2.33

a) There's a rug on the floor.
b) There's a lamp in the corner.
c) There's a magazine under the coffee table.
d) There's a plant next to the sofa.
e) There are some cushions on the sofa.
f) There are some pictures on the wall, above the sofa.

🔊 **2.34**

a) 'Is there a computer in your living room?' 'Yes, there is.' `No, there isn't.'
b) 'Are there any plants in your kitchen?' 'Yes, there are.' 'No, there aren't.'
c) 'Are there any pictures in your bedroom?' 'Yes, there are.' 'No, there aren't.'
d) 'Is there a carpet in your bathroom?' 'Yes, there is.' 'No, there isn't.'
e) 'Is there a television in your bathroom?' 'Yes, there is.' 'No, there isn't.'
f) 'Are there any cushions in your bedroom?' 'Yes, there are.' 'No, there aren't.'

🔊 **2.36**

a) I live in the city.
b) I live on a hill.
c) I live near the sea.
d) I live in the mountains.
e) I live in the country.
f) I live on an island.
g) I live near a river.
h) I live in a small village.
i) I live on the coast.
j) I live on the top floor.
k) I live near a lake.
l) I live near a park.

Unit 10

🔊 **2.40**

a) Proteins: cheese, eggs, meat, chicken, seafood, fish
b) Vegetables: a cauliflower, peppers, tomatoes, mushrooms, beans, garlic, carrots, onions, olive oil
c) Fruit: a melon, pears, oranges, a lemon, strawberries, grapes, bananas, apples
d) Carbohydrates: bread, potatoes, cakes, cereal, rice, pasta

🔊 **2.42**

a) bread   c) potato
b) garlic   d) cereal

🔊 **2.43**

a) 'Are there any mushrooms in photo *b*?' 'Yes, there are.' 'No, there aren't.'
b) 'Is there any cheese in photo *c*?' 'Yes, there is.' 'No, there isn't.'
c) 'Is there a cauliflower in photo *b*?' 'Yes, there is.' 'No, there isn't.'
d) 'Is there any pasta in photo *d*?' 'Yes, there is.' 'No, there isn't.'
e) 'Are there any bananas in photo *d*?' 'Yes, there are.' 'No, there aren't.'
f) 'Is there any bread in photo *a*?' 'Yes, there is.' 'No, there isn't.'

🔊 **2.45**

(A = Alan; K = Kathryn)
A: I want to lose weight but I love my food. How do you stay so slim?
K: I follow the food-combining rules.
A: Food-combining? What's that?
K: Well, for example, I never eat protein and carbohydrates together.
A: What? Do you mean you never eat steak and chips?

K: No, because steak is protein and chips are carbohydrates.
A: Oh. What about fish and rice. That's healthy.
K: No, fish is protein and rice is carbohydrate. Fish and vegetables is OK.
A: Well, how about my favourite meal – spaghetti bolognese with fruit salad for dessert.
K: No, sorry. There's meat in bolognese and spaghetti is carbohydrate. And you can't eat fruit as a dessert.
A: Oh dear. I don't like this. My favourite diet is the 'seafood' diet.
K: Oh, what's that?
A: When you see food, you eat it.
K&A: Ha ha ha.

🔊 **2.46**

a) 'How much bread is there?' 'There isn't much.'
b) 'How many eggs are there?' 'There are a lot.'
c) 'How many lemons are there?' 'There aren't any.'
d) 'How much meat is there?' 'There's a lot.'
e) 'How much milk is there?' 'There isn't any.'
f) 'How many peppers are there?' 'There aren't many.'

🔊 **2.47**

We had a delicious meal last weekend. It was my brother's 18th birthday, and the whole family went out. We had a meal in an Italian restaurant. It's called Mario's, and they do fantastic pizzas there. There were fifteen of us – me, my brother, our parents, our grandmother, our cousins and my brother's best friends. I sat next to my grandmother, but she fell asleep after two glasses of wine. Everybody had pizza. The restaurant made my brother a special birthday cake, and we all sang 'Happy Birthday' – I think he was a bit embarrassed. The cake was delicious, and we had some champagne too. I think we stayed in the restaurant for nearly three hours. I didn't get home till 1.00 a.m. It was a really good evening.

Unit 11

🔊 **2.50**

a) Will is Sue's son.
b) Nancy is Simon's daughter.
c) Gus is Zainab's brother.
d) Albert is Jem's father.

🔊 **2.51**

a) Will has a shaved head. He's very good-looking.
b) Jem has short, straight hair with blond highlights.
c) Sue has dark hair and green eyes.
d) Albert has short, grey hair.
e) Gus has dark brown eyes and short hair.
f) Nancy has short, curly hair. She's very sweet.

g) Zainab has medium-length, dark hair. She has a lovely smile.
h) Simon has very curly hair.

🔊 **2.54**

A: Singular nouns
a coat, a jacket, a shirt, a suit, a tie, a sweater, a top, a tracksuit, a T-shirt, a belt, a hat, a ring
B: Plural nouns
a pair of boots, a pair of shoes, a pair of trainers, a pair of socks, a pair of underpants, a pair of trousers, a pair of jeans, a pair of sunglasses

🔊 **2.55**

(I = Interviewer; S = Stuart)
I: Stuart, you really like buying clothes, don't you?
S: Oh yes, I love it.
I: How many items of clothing do you have?
S: Well … I have 350 shirts. I wear three or four different shirts every day.
I: Goodness. 350 shirts! Er … who does the washing?
S: My wife does the washing, and I do the ironing. Then I have 200 suits. I like bright colours – red, blue and green.
I: Mm, I see.
S: Then I have 150 pairs of trousers.
I: 150 pairs of trousers?
S: Yes, and 125 pairs of shoes.
I: Stuart, why do you have so many clothes?
S: Well, it's my hobby. Some people spend lots of money on cars, or holidays.
I don't have a car, and I never go on holiday. I buy clothes.

🔊 **2.57**

Good evening. I'm Ross White and I'm standing outside the Kodak Theatre in Hollywood. I'm waiting for the big stars to arrive for this year's Oscars ceremony. And here comes Keira Knightley. She's wearing a beautiful red dress.
Oh, wow – there's Charlize Theron. She's talking to the photographers. Oh, and what's she doing now? She's turning around. Hi, Charlize! Good luck! Oh, what a gorgeous woman!
Right, Jake Gyllenhaal's arriving now. He's wearing a black bow tie. Oh, he's so good-looking! And he's smiling at everybody.

🔊 **2.58**

a) 'Are you wearing jeans?' 'Yes, I am.' 'No, I'm not.'
b) 'Are you sitting next to a window?' 'Yes, I am.' 'No, I'm not.'
c) 'Is your teacher standing up?' 'Yes, she is.' 'No, she isn't.'
d) 'Is the traffic making a noise?' 'Yes, it is.' 'No, it isn't.'
e) 'Are you all wearing watches?' 'Yes, we are.' 'No, we aren't.'
f) 'Are the birds singing outside?' 'Yes, they are.' 'No, they aren't.'

Unit 12

🔊 2.62

Karyn had a good job but she loved shopping. She used her credit card a lot and soon she had a huge debt. Then she lost her job. She couldn't pay her bills, so she started a website and asked people for money. After five months she paid her credit card bill. Then she wrote a book about her experience.

🔊 2.63

a) I never save money. I always spend all my money.
b) I spent a lot of money last weekend.
c) My salary was lower five years ago.
d) I always pay my bills on time.
e) I never use my credit card to buy things on the internet.

🔊 2.64

Short adjectives: bigger, cleaner, faster, happier, older, richer
Long adjectives:, more beautiful, more important, more interesting
Irregular forms: better

🔊 2.65

a) I'm taller than Alex.
b) I'm older than Carole.
c) My handwriting is worse than Gina's.
d) My mobile phone is smaller than Eddie's.
e) My house is further from the school than Ian's.
f) My pen was more expensive than Kerry's.

🔊 2.67

a) One million, two hundred and fifty thousand, six hundred and twenty dollars.
b) Eighty-five thousand, five hundred and ninety dollars.
c) Eleven million, three hundred and two thousand, six hundred and fifty dollars.
d) Sixty-five thousand, two hundred and eight dollars.

🔊 2.68

1 The most valuable watch is by Patek Phillippe. It's made of 18-carat gold and is worth $11,302,650.
2 The most valuable pair of jeans are an original pair of 115-year-old Levis. A Japanese collector bought them on the internet in 2005. The jeans cost $65,208.
3 The most valuable dress is the dress worn by Marilyn Monroe when she sang 'Happy Birthday, Mr President' to JF Kennedy in 1962. In 1999 a collector bought the dress for $1,250,620.
4 The most valuable pair of shoes are a pair of shoes worn by Emperor Bokassa of the Central African Republic in 1977. The shoes cost $85,590.

🔊 2.69

a) Who's the youngest?
b) Who's the oldest?
c) Who's the most interesting?
d) Who's the luckiest?

e) Who's the worst driver?
f) Who's the best cook?

Review C

🔊 3.01

A: armchair, curly, garlic, lemon
B: beautiful, interesting, salary, vegetable
C: moustache, tattoo
D: banana, expensive, important, potato

🔊 3.03

(R = Receptionist; L = Lara)
R: The Fat Cat. Can I help you?
L: Yes, I'd like to make a reservation, please.
R: Of course. What day?
L: Friday 15th August.
R: Is that for lunch or dinner?
L: Dinner.
R: I'm sorry. We have tables for lunch, but there aren't any tables for dinner on the 15th. There's a big party that night. The chef's getting married.
L: Oh. It's my birthday.
R: Would you like a different day?
L: What about Saturday – Saturday 16th August?
R: For dinner?
L: Yes.
R: Yes. We have some tables for dinner on Saturday.
L: Great.
R: How many people?
L: Six. Do you have a window table?
R: Sorry?
L: Do you have a table near the window, with a view of the river?
R: Certainly. What time would you like, seven thirty or nine o'clock?
L: Er, nine, I think.
R: And what's your name?
L: Lara Gluck.
R: Can you spell that, please?
L: L–A–R–A G–L–U–C–K.
R: OK. That's a window table for six people at 9.00 p.m. on Saturday 16th August.
L: Thank you. Er, is there a dress code?
R: Yes. No jeans, and we ask men to wear a jacket and tie.
L: OK. Oh, and can I pay by credit card?
R: Yes, that's no problem. See you on Saturday.

Unit 13

🔊 3.05

It's time for *Hidden talents*!
  Hi everybody. In *Hidden talents* today we look at some of the things you didn't know about your favourite stars.
  First up we have Bruce Willis, our favourite Hollywood actor. Did you know that Bruce can play the harmonica? It's true!
  Next is Bono from our favourite band in the world, U2. Even rock stars relax, and Mr Bono can play chess really well.
  Shakira has everything – she's beautiful and talented and she can speak Spanish, English, Italian, Arabic and Portuguese. Wow. Five languages!

And finally what about the queen of pop, Madonna? Well, she loves horses and she can ride really well. She has some beautiful horses at her big country house in England. And now …

🔊 3.06

a) 'Can you play the harmonica?'
   'Yes, I can.' 'No, I can't.'
b) 'Can your father play chess?'
   'Yes, he can.' 'No, he can't.'
c) 'Can you speak five languages?'
   'Yes, I can.' 'No, I can't.'
d) 'Can your mother ride a horse?'
   'Yes, she can.' 'No, she can't.'
e) 'Can you dance flamenco?'
   'Yes, I can.' 'No, I can't.'
f) 'Can your parents ski?'
   'Yes, they can.' 'No, they can't.'

🔊 3.08

a) I eat my food very slowly.
b) I drive my car quite fast.
c) I play the guitar very badly.
d) I spend my money very carefully.
e) I play the drums very loudly.
f) I don't eat my soup very quietly.
g) I do my homework very happily.
h) I don't speak English very well.

🔊 3.10

a) He travels all the time.
b) He sleeps for five or six hours a night.
c) He practises for more than five hours a day.
d) He buys new shoes every month.
e) He eats three times a day.
f) He calls his family every day.

🔊 3.11

1 three times a day
2 every day
3 twice a week
4 every two weeks
5 once a month
6 four times a year

🔊 3.12

a) How often do you travel?
b) How often do you buy new shoes?
c) How often do you call your family?

🔊 3.13

a) confident – 3: You are very sure of yourself.
b) generous – 1: You give a lot of time and/or money to people.
c) selfish – 5: You don't think about other people.
d) sensible – 6: You never do stupid things.
e) serious – 4: You think about things and don't laugh much.
f) shy – 2: You are nervous about meeting people.

🔊 3.14

a) 2: 'I have a bad back.'
b) 4: 'I don't have time.'
c)   1: 'I'm really tired.'
d) 5: 'I have a cold.'
e) 6: 'I have a headache.'
f) 3: 'I don't have any money.'

Unit 14

💿 3.17

a) How many televisions do you have in your house?
b) How many hours of TV do you watch every day?
c) When do you usually switch on the television? When do you switch it off?
d) How many different channels can you get on your television?
e) What's your favourite TV programme?
f) What's on TV this evening?

💿 3.18

1
A: Next question. On the border of which two South American countries can you find the Iguaçu Falls?
B: Oh. Um. Mm, I know this one. Is it Argentina and Chile? No – Argentina and Brazil.
A: Is that your final answer?
B: Yes.
A: Are you sure?
B: Um, yes.
A: It's the correct answer – YOU'VE JUST WON £125,000!!!

2
Police arrested two men after they attempted to rob a bank in the centre of London this morning. The men were armed, but nobody was hurt.

3
C: Oh, hello, Mr Jones. How are you today?
D: Oh, can't complain. Here, have you heard about that Andy Clifford?
C: No, what?
D: Well, I've heard he's going to get married to … Rachel Smedley.
C: Rachel Smedley – no!

4
E: Well, Michael, you've had a very successful career in the film business. Did you always want to be a movie star?
F: Not exactly. I grew up on a farm in the Mid-West and when I was a young boy all I wanted to be was a farmer like my dad.
E: So what made you change your mind?
F: Well, it was …

5
The shark is the king of the sea. It fills people with fear. But that's not the whole story. Yes, some kinds of shark are dangerous, but most of them are harmless and shy. Take the Spotted Wobbegong – not a beautiful specimen – quite ugly in fact …

6
BB: This is Big Brother. The nominations for eviction are … Vicky!
V: Oh … I knew it
BB: And … Clyde!

💿 3.21

a) I want to travel around the world.
b) I want to live in a foreign country.
c) I don't want to get married.
d) I'd like to have lots of children.
e) I wouldn't like to be famous.
f) I hope to retire before I'm sixty.

💿 3.22

(I = Interviewer; L = Lynne)
I: Lynne, congratulations!
L: Thank you. I can't believe it.
I: What's the first thing you're going to do when you leave the *Big Brother* house?
L: I'm going to have a big party. I missed my friends so much.
I: Ah. What are you going to do with the money?
L: I'm going to buy a house for my mum.
I: Oh, that's great. Which *Big Brother* housemates are you going to see again?
L: There are some people I'd like to see again, but I'm not going to see Sheryl and Josh – they were horrible to me.
I: Oh yes, that's true … But what about Eddie? You became really good – er – friends in the House. Are you going to see Eddie again?
L: Yes, of course we're going to see one another. I really miss him.
I: Finally, Lynne, what are your plans for the future?
L: Well, first I'm going to go out and spend some money. Then I want to start my singing career. I'm going to record a CD. I'd also like to be a interviewer on TV.
I: Oh, well, good luck.

💿 3.23

a) 'Is she going to have a big party?' 'Yes, she is.' 'No, she isn't.'
b) Is she going to buy a house for her mum?' 'Yes, she is.' 'No, she isn't.'
c) 'Is she going to see Sheryl and Josh?' 'Yes, she is.' 'No, she isn't.'
d) 'Is she going to see Eddie?' 'Yes, she is.' 'No, she isn't.'
e) 'Is she going to go out and spend some money?' 'Yes, she is.' 'No, she isn't.'
f) 'Is she going to record a CD?' 'Yes, she is.' 'No, she isn't.'

💿 3.24

a) I'm going to do more exercise.
b) I'm going to eat healthier food.
c) I'm going to save more money.
d) I'm going to spend more time with my family.
e) I'm not going to watch so much TV.
f) I'm not going to arrive late for appointments.

💿 3.26

(M = Max; J = Juliet)
M: OK, Juliet. So what's your favourite TV programme?
J: My favourite TV programme? *Desperate Housewives.*
M: What sort of programme is it?
J: It's a drama, but it's funny too. So I suppose it's a comedy drama.
M: Who are the main characters?

J: There are five women – Susan, Bree, um Lynette, Gabrielle and Edie. They all live in the same street and they're all friends. Well, sometimes they're friends.
M: What's it about?
J: It's about their lives.
M: Who's your favourite character?
J: Hm, I like Bree. She's crazy.
M: What day is it on?
J: Wednesdays.
M: Did you see it last Wednesday?
J: Yes, of course.
M: What happened?
J: Oh, um, Bree met a new man.
M: Oh. Why do you like it?
J: I like the humour – it's very dark. Anyway, what's your favourite programme.
M: Um, *Who wants to be a Millionaire?*

Unit 15

💿 3.30

1 Steve
I love shopping. I've been to Hong Kong, and there are fantastic shops there. But my favourite place to shop is the Grand Bazaar in Istanbul. It's amazing.
I also love beaches. So I've been to the Seychelles and I've been to some Greek islands. But I haven't been to Hawaii. I'm getting married next year and I want to go there for my honeymoon.

2 Ben
I don't like cities – there are too many cars and people everywhere. I love going to wild places. I've been to the Amazon – that was amazing. I love deserts, but I haven't been to the Sahara yet. That's my next trip.

3 Rose
I enjoy walking. So I've been to Tuscany, the Loire Valley and the North Island in New Zealand. I also love historical places. I've been to Petra in Jordan and the Great Wall of China. One day, I'd like to visit Angkor Wat in Cambodia.

💿 3.32

a) I've been to Tuscany.
b) I haven't been to Istanbul.
c) He's been to Hawaii.
d) He hasn't been to Petra.

💿 3.33

a) 'Have you ever been to Angkor Wat?' 'Yes, I have.' 'No, I haven't.'
b) 'Has your father ever been to London?' 'Yes, he has.' 'No, he hasn't.'
c) 'Have you ever been to a big pop concert?' 'Yes, I have.' 'No, I haven't.'
d) 'Has your mother ever been to a football match?' 'Yes, she has.' 'No, she hasn't.'
e) 'Have you and your family ever been to Paris?' 'Yes, we have.' 'No, we haven't.'
f) 'Have students in the class ever been to your house?' 'Yes, they have.' 'No, they haven't.'

3.35

A: break, broke, broken; speak, spoke, spoken; do, did, done; swim, swam, swum

B: shake, shook, shaken; take, took, taken; fly, flew, flown; know, knew, known

C: give, gave, given; drive, drove, driven; say, said, said; read, read, read

3.37

(W = Will; R = Rick)

W: Hello.

R: Hi, Will!

W: Rick! …

R: How are you, Will?

W: I'm fine. Hey, where are you?

R: In Ecuador.

W: Ecuador? Amazing. How's it going?

R: Really well. I'm enjoying the job. I've seen a lot of South America.

W: Where have you been?

R: Argentina, Chile, Peru, Ecuador … I've driven 12,000 kilometres in the last six months.

W: 12,000 kilometres! What's the best place you've been to?

R: I've seen so many beautiful places – but I think Patagonia was the best.

W: Have you been to Brazil?

R: Yeah, I have,

W: When did you go?

R: In February. I went to the Carnival in Rio.

W: Amazing!

R: Yeah, I met some great people in Rio. We had parties on the beach. It was really good fun.

W: What about the people on the trips?

R: Well, I've had a few problems.

W: Oh dear. What happened?

R: Well, one girl lost her passport. And a man got ill – I took him to hospital.

W: Ah. Have *you* had any accidents?

R: No, no, I haven't had any accidents.

W: Oh, good.

R: But … I have had a few problems with the police.

W: Really? What happened?

R: Oh, it's a long story – I'll write to you.

W: OK. Have you met any nice people?

R: Yes – lots of nice people. I met a very nice woman last month in Peru. Her name's Ana and …

W: Really? Tell me more. … Rick? RICK? Oh no, he's gone.

3.39

a) When did you go? Who did you go with?

b) When did you move? Where did you move to?

c) When did you lose it? What did you do?

d) What did you win? When did you win it?

e) When did you see it? Which one did you see?

3.40

My oldest friend is Simon. We first met at school – secondary school. We were thirteen or fourteen– I can't remember exactly. We became friends because we laugh at the same things. Simon is very funny. Now he's a doctor. He's married and he lives in London. I see him a few times a year. The last time I saw him was on his birthday. We went out for a lovely meal. His wife and my girlfriend get on really well. My best memory of Simon is a holiday we had together in the USA. We were twenty-three, and it was the year we finished university. We drove from Chicago to Los Angeles. It was fantastic.

Unit 16

3.44

a) He lives about fifty kilometres from his work.

b) She lives about seven kilometres from her work.

c) It takes her two hours to get to work.

d) It takes him forty minutes to get to work.

e) He goes along the coast and through the National Park.

f) She goes down Sukhumvit Road and through the city centre.

3.45

a) I go down the stairs.

b) I go out of my apartment.

c) I go across the street.

d) I go along the river.

e) I go past some shops.

f) I go up a hill.

g) I go through the park.

h) I go over a bridge.

i) I go into my office.

3.46

a) Where do you start from?

b) Who do you travel with?

c) What do you talk about?

d) What kind of music do you listen to?

e) What kind of scenery do you go through?

f) What kind of buildings do you go past?

3.48

a) /ɑː/: car, start, past

b) /ɜː/: world, first, turn

c) /ɔː/: fourth, saw, walk

d) /uː/: blue, two, through

3.49

(P = Presenter; K = Kelly)

P: Welcome to *Amazing Journeys*. Today's programme is about a man who has travelled round the world by bicycle. Kelly, what can you tell us about Heinz Stücke?

K: Well, Heinz Stücke has actually been round the world ten times by bicycle.

P: Ten times?! When did he start his journey?

K: He started his journey in 1962. He left Germany when he was twenty-two years old. At first, he planned to travel only for a few years.

P: What happened?

K: Well, he forgot to stop!

P: How many countries has he visited?

K: Two hundred and eleven countries. He's filled fifteen passports.

P: Fifteen passports! And what sort of bicycle does he have??

K: It's a big, heavy bicycle – it weighs twenty-five kilos. He has very strong legs!

P: I can imagine. Where does he sleep?

K: He usually sleeps in a tent.

P: And how does he make money?

K: He sells postcards of his trip.

P: I see. Where is he now?

K: At the moment, he's cycling along the south coast of England.

P: So, when is he going to finish his journey?

K: I don't know. Maybe never.

3.50

Heinz Stücke has been round the world ten times by bicycle. He started his journey forty-five years ago. He left Germany when he was twenty-two years old.

He has visited two hundred and eleven countries and he has filled fifteen passports.

His bicycle weighs twenty-five kilos. He usually sleeps in a tent and he makes money by selling postcards of his trip.

At the moment, he is cycling along the south coast of England.

When is he going to finish his journey? He doesn't know. Maybe never!

3.52

Last spring, I went to Tuscany, one of my favourite places in Italy. I went with my friend, Julia. We had a little white Mazda. I drove and Julia read the map. I can't read maps.

One day we decided to drive from Siena to Saturnia. We left Siena in the morning, and it was already sunny and hot. We drove through green fields and hills. Tuscany is so beautiful. We stopped in a small village on top of a hill. We visited an old church and bought some wine. Then we continued our drive through the Tuscan hills and arrived in Saturnia in the afternoon. There are hot springs in Saturnia, so we parked near a waterfall and went swimming in the river. It was amazing.

3.54

a)

A: Hi. Where are you?

B: I'm at the roundabout.

A: OK. Go down College Road and take the third turning on the right. That's Church Street.

B: OK.

A: Our house is opposite the church.

B: OK, see you in ten minutes.

b)

C: Hello.

D: Hi. I'm at the roundabout.

C: OK. Go down London Road and take the second turning on the left. That's Henley Street.

D: OK.

C: Then go straight on and take the first turning on the right.

D: OK.

C: There's a pub on the left. We're there.

D: Great. Get me a beer!

c)

E: Hello.
F: Hello. I'm lost.
E: Oh dear. Where are you?
F: At the roundabout.
E: OK. Go down Abingdon Road and take the second turning on the left.
F: OK.
E: Then go to the end of New Street and turn right. There's a bank on the right, and our house is opposite. It's number 21.
F: OK, thanks. See you soon.

Review D

🔘 3.56

A: channel, desert, selfish
B: carefully, generous, sensible
C: dessert, respect, weekend
D: adventure, appointment, koala
E: competitive, experience, spectacular

🔘 3.58

(I = Interviewer; J = Jasmine)

I: Good morning. I'm Bill Smiley, and today I'm talking to Jasmine Smith from the organisation, *Blind Hope*. Welcome, Jasmine.
J: Thank you.
I: Jasmine, you and your husband John started *Blind Hope* last year to help blind children in other countries. Two weeks ago, something fantastic happened. Tell us about it.
J: Yes. Someone gave $1 million to *Blind Hope*. I can't say who gave us the money, but it was a very rich film star. We were so excited!
I: And now you're organising a very special trip to Kenya.
J: Yes, that's right. We'd like to help blind children all around the world, and we're starting in Kenya. *Blind Hope* is going to use some of the money to open a school there.
I: And now, Jasmine, I believe you are looking for people from this area who want to go to Kenya next year.
J: Yes, I'd like to find twelve people to help build the school with me.
I: What sort of people?
J: Well, we're looking for people who are friendly, confident, and who can work well with other people. We don't want people who only want to have a good time and travel. We want sensible people, because this is a serious job. And it's hard work. You need to be full of energy. It isn't a holiday!
I: I see. And what are *Blind Hope*'s plans for the future, Jasmine?
J: *Blind Hope* has big plans, Bill. Every journey starts with a single step. We hope to build one school in a different country every year.
I: Wow! Good luck, Jasmine. It's a great plan!
J: Thank you.
I: If you would like to go to Kenya, or if you want to give money to *Blind Hope*, you can find the details on our website at www …

Phonetic symbols

Single vowels

/ɪ/	fish	/fɪʃ/
/iː/	bean	/biːn/
/ʊ/	foot	/fʊt/
/uː/	shoe	/ʃuː/
/e/	egg	/eg/
/ə/	mother	/ɛmʌðə/
/ɜː/	word	/wɜːd/
/ɔː/	talk	/tɔːk/
/æ/	back	/bæk/
/ʌ/	bus	/bʌs/
/ɑː/	arm	/ɑːm/
/ɒ/	top	/tɒp/

Diphthongs

/ɪə/	ear	/ɪə/
/eɪ/	face	/feɪs/
/ʊə/	tourist	/ɛtʊərɪst/
/ɔɪ/	boy	/bɔɪ/
/əʊ/	nose	/nəʊz/
/eə/	hair	/heə/
/aɪ/	eye	/aɪ/
/aʊ/	mouth	/maʊθ/

Consonants

/p/	pen	/pen/
/b/	bag	/bæg/
/t/	tea	/tiː/
/d/	dog	/dɒg/
/tʃ/	chip	/tʃɪp/
/dʒ/	jazz	/dʒæz/
/k/	cake	/keɪk/
/g/	girl	/gɜːl/
/f/	film	/fɪlm/
/v/	verb	/vɜːb/
/θ/	thing	/θɪŋ/
/ð/	these	/ðiːz/
/s/	snake	/sneɪk/
/z/	zoo	/zuː/
/ʃ/	shop	/ʃɒp/
/ʒ/	television	/ɛtelɪvɪʒən/
/m/	map	/mæp/
/n/	name	/neɪm/
/ŋ/	ring	/rɪŋ/
/h/	house	/haʊs/
/l/	leg	/leg/
/r/	road	/rəʊd/
/w/	wine	/waɪn/
/j/	yes	/jes/

Stress

Word stress is shown by underlining the stressed syllable: water, amazing, Japanese.

Letters of the alphabet

/eɪ/	/iː/	/e/	/aɪ/	/əʊ/	/uː/	/ɑː/
Aa	Bb	Ff	Ii	Oo	Qq	Rr
Hh	Cc	Ll	Yy		Uu	
Jj	Dd	Mm			Ww	
Kk	Ee	Nn				
	Gg	Ss				
	Pp	Xx				
	Tt	Zz				
	Vv					

Irregular verbs

Infinitive	Past simple	Past participle
be	was/were	been
beat	beat	beaten
become	became	become
begin	began	begun
bend	bent	bent
bet	bet	bet
bite	bit	bitten
blow	blew	blown
break	broke	broken
bring	brought /brɔːt/	brought /brɔːt/
build /bɪld/	built /bɪlt/	built /bɪlt/
burn	burnt/burned	burnt/burned
burst	burst	burst
buy /baɪ/	bought /bɔːt/	bought /bɔːt/
can	could /kʊd/	(been able)
catch	caught /kɔːt/	caught /kɔːt/
choose	chose	chosen
come	came	come
cost	cost	cost
cut	cut	cut
deal /diːl/	dealt /delt/	dealt /delt/
dig	dug	dug
do	did	done
draw	drew	drawn
dream	dreamt/dreamed	dreamt/dreamed
drink	drank	drunk
drive	drove	driven
eat	ate	eaten
fall	fell	fallen
feed	fed	fed
feel	felt	felt
fight	fought /fɔːt/	fought /fɔːt/
find	found	found
fly	flew	flown
forget	forgot	forgotten
forgive	forgave	forgiven
freeze	froze	frozen
get	got	got
give	gave	given
go	went	gone/been
grow	grew	grown
hang	hung/hanged	hung/hanged
have	had	had
hear	heard /hɜːd/	heard /hɜːd/
hide	hid	hidden
hit	hit	hit
hold	held	held
hurt /hɜːt/	hurt /hɜːt/	hurt /hɜːt/
keep	kept	kept
kneel	knelt/kneeled	knelt/kneeled
know	knew /njuː/	known
lay	laid	laid
lead	led	led
learn	learnt	learnt
leave	left	left
lend	lent	lent
let	let	let

Infinitive	Past simple	Past participle
lie	lay	lain
light	lit/lighted	lit/lighted
lose	lost	lost
make	made	made
mean	meant /ment/	meant /ment/
meet	met	met
must	had to	(had to)
pay	paid	paid
put	put	put
read	read /red/	read /red/
ride	rode	ridden
ring	rang	rung
rise	rose	risen
run	ran	run
say	said /sed/	said /sed/
see	saw /sɔː/	seen
sell	sold	sold
send	sent	sent
set	set	set
shake	shook	shaken
shine	shone	shone
shoot	shot	shot
show	showed	shown
shrink	shrank	shrunk
shut	shut	shut
sing	sang	sung
sink	sank	sunk
sit	sat	sat
sleep	slept	slept
slide	slid	slid
smell	smelt/smelled	smelt/smelled
speak	spoke	spoken
spell	spelt/spelled	spelt/spelled
spend	spent	spent
spill	spilt/spilled	spilt/spilled
split	split	split
spoil	spoilt/spoiled	spoilt/spoiled
spread	spread	spread
stand	stood	stood
steal	stole	stolen
stick	stuck	stuck
swear	swore	sworn
swell	swelled	swollen/swelled
swim	swam	swum
take	took /tʊk/	taken
teach	taught /tɔːt/	taught /tɔːt/
tear	tore	torn
tell	told	told
think	thought /θɔːt/	thought /θɔːt/
throw	threw	thrown
understand	understood	understood
wake	woke	woken
wear	wore /wɔː/	worn
win	won /wʌn/	won /wʌn/
write	wrote	written

Macmillan Education
4 Crinan Street,
London N1 9XW
A division of Springer Nature Ltd
Companies and representatives throughout the world

ISBN 978-1-4050-8594-6

Text © Sue Kay & Vaughan Jones 2007
Design and illustration © Springer Nature Ltd

First published 2007

Review units by Peter Maggs and Catherine Smith
Project development by Desmond O'Sullivan, Quality Outcomes Limited
Designed by 320 Design Limited
Photographic research and editorial by Sally Cole, Perseverance Works Limited
Illustrated by Beach pp 6, 9, 15, 21, 27, 32, 37, 39, 43, 49, 55, 63, 65, 69, 71, 77, 81, 83, 93, 99, 105, 111, 118, 123; Cyrus Deboo p 107; Ed McLachlan pp 8, 14, 20, 28, 36, 40, 42, 46, 48, 54, 57, 64, 70, 76, 79, 82, 84, 92, 98, 101, 104, 110, 112, 127, 129, 131, 133; Montana Forbes p 22; Andy Parker p 94; Gavin Reece pp 119, 124; Tobatron p 61; Lucy Truman p 63; Adrian Valencia p 85
Cover design by Andrew Oliver

Authors' acknowledgements
We would like to thank all our students and colleagues at the Oxford English Centre in Oxford. Your help has been invaluable. Particular thanks go to our OEC students who took part in the New Inside Out Elementary DVD and helped to make it such a good one.
We would also like to thank our teacher colleagues around the world who are using Inside Out – your feedback has helped us identify what we should keep and what we could improve. Particular thanks go to the following people: Sean Wordingham at the British Council in Chiang Mai; Maya Neishtadt, Yana Orlitskaya, Svetlana Babaeva, Professor Tatiana Shepelenk, Natalia Potapova, Suriya Shukurova, Irina Kruglova, Gillian Davidson, Madina Fiodorova, Professor Olga Kolykhalova, Natalia Kolesnikova and Professor Olga Kaznina (Moscow); Peter Tamkin and Phil Hopkins (English Language Centre, Brighton); as well as the staff and students at Oxford House College (London), St Giles College (London), EF (London), Aspect ILA (London), Regent School (London), Wimbledon School of English (London) and Francis King School of English (London).
We are especially grateful to Peter Maggs and Catherine Smith for the wonderful New Inside Out Workbook as well as their Student's Book review units, and to Helena Gomm, Caroline Brown, Peter Maggs and Chris Dawson for their important contributions to the New Inside Out Teacher's Book. We're also grateful to Scott Thornbury for allowing us to use extracts from his excellent book, An A–Z of ELT. At Macmillan Education, we would like to thank Kate Melliss, Rafael Alarcon-Gaeta, Jemma Harrison, Karen White, Balvir Koura, Guy Jackson, Candice Renault and Stephanie Parker.
We would also like to thank Sally Cole (freelance photo researcher), Alyson Maskell, Celia Bingham and Xanthe Sturt Taylor (freelance editors), as well as James Richardson and Jeff Capel (freelance audio producers).
Jackie Hill and Kim Williams – our wonderfully talented freelance designers – continue to work their magic. We constantly marvel at how they manage to bring our text to life. Inside Out would not be the stylish course it is without them, or without Andrew Oliver's fabulous cover design.
Many thanks also go to the Macmillan production and marketing teams, and in particular to Jo Greig and Matt Kay whose enthusiasm and encouragement have been such a support.
As always, our biggest thanks go to Des O'Sullivan (freelance project developer). It's a joy and a rare privilege to work with such a consummate professional. We consider ourselves extremely fortunate.
Last but not least, we are so grateful to our families for their ongoing support and understanding.

The authors and publishers are grateful for permission to reprint the following copyright material: Extract from www.savekaryn.com, reprinted by permission of RLR Associates Ltd on behalf of Karyn Bosnak.
These materials may contain links for third party websites. We have no control over, and are not responsible for, the contents of such third party websites. Please use care when accessing them.
The authors and publishers would like to thank the following for permission to reproduce their photographs: Actionplus/B.Ainslee p44(f); Alamy/J.Waterman p5(b), N.Price p11(a), Uripos p12(b), P.Solloway p12(c), All Star Picture Library pp26(t), 88(1), TNT Magazine p100(tr), Jake Norton p102(t), Peter Horree p102(bl), W.Bibikow p106(tl), W.Manning Photography p106(tr), M.Brivio p106(b), P.Doyle pp59(tr), 114(l); Anglia/B.Hobbs p73; Corbis/M.Prince p11(c), J.Craigmyle p11(c), R.Lewine p11(b), T.Tadder p12(d), T.Reed p23(m), RCWW Inc. p24(l), F.Trapper p26(mt), Reuters pp26(mb), (b), 35, 38(b), 41(m), 41(b), 84(r), D.Raymer p31, S.Marcus p34(t), P.Turnley p34(m), R.Hellestad p38(t), S.McLaughlin p44(b), H.Trygg p44(g), C.Carroll p44(bl), J.Springer Collection p52, M.Anzuoni p58(c), R.Folkks p58(a), B.Kraft p58(b), Sygma p58(3), S.Frink p59(mr), R.Landau p59(br), Bettmann Archive p80(d), J.Schmelzer p85, J.Bilic p86(b), S.Frink p87(l), G.Baden p87(t), B.Harris p87(m), D.Munoz p88(3), S.Cardinale p88(2), L.O'Connor p88(4), Creasource p89, R.Gomez p95(a), E.Bock pp95(b), 96, D.Galante p95(c), B.Pepone p95(d), M.Watson p95(e), A.Scott p97(l), Imagesource p100(l), J.Feingersh p102(tl), Grace p102(bl), Troy p107, U.Wiesmeier p115(b), DK Library p45; Empics/D.Ockenden p86(t); Getty pp115(t), p58(br), S.Murphy p4, Stock4B p5(d), H.Sorensen p5(c), S.Stafford p5(a), A.Caulfield p7, Fotos International p10, D.Arsenault p11(a), Longview p12(e), C.Wilhelm p12(f), E.O'Brien p18(l), J.Knowles p18(r), Giantstep Inc. p19, Z.Shroff p22(l), C.Gullung p22(r), W.Packert p23(l), R.Ross p23(r), M.Harris p25, J.Tisne p30(l), E.Nathan p20(tr), Z.Smith p30(mr), S.Indermaur Photography p30(b), B.Wilson p33, A.Mo p34(b), R.Scorza p41(1), F.Caffrey p41(l), M.Cosslett p44(c), D.Sacks p44(d), J.Nicholson p44(a), D.Vervits p44(br), C.Allegri p47(l), N.Kamm p58(bl), M.Cardy p59(tl), G.George p68, P.Harvey p69, F.Harrison pp75(m), (r), F.Micelotta p75(l), P.Cade p78(b), E.Agostini p84(l), Handout p86(m), DreamPictures p86(r), N.Dolding p87(b), C.Harvey p91, D.Anschutz p95(f), China Tourism Press p100(b), A.Murrell p108(t), H.Merten p109(1), M.Epstein p109(2), R.Johnston p109(3), J.Wyman p109(4), M.Mehlig p113, J.Feingersh p115(mr), Cayman p115(ml); A.Gramer p32; Guinness World Records p80(b); Idols Licensing p28; Masterfile/G.Shelley p109(b); Panos Pictures/C.Penn p114(r); Photolibrary pp12(g), 17, 24(r), 44(e), 47(r), 67, 103; Reuters/F.Paredes p90; Rex Features pp51(l), (r), 80(a), 80(c), 97(r), 108(b), D.Stone p5(f), Conrad p16, Sipa Press p58(tl), Roderick Angle Photography p74; Science Photo Library/J.Cole p12(h); The Kobal Collection/Plunge Pictures p47(b). Hotel Hurricane with kind permission of www.hotelhurricane.com p53; Emirates Palace Hotel pp60(b), 61; Noble House Hotel p60(t).
Commissioned photography by Haddon Davies pp50, 66, and Dean Ryan p6.
Photographs on p72 with kind permission of Sue Kay and Vaughan Jones; photo on p78(t) with kind permission of Karyn.

Printed and bound in Poland by Dimograf

2018
020